P9-AFR-063

You can't buy love like that

You can't buy love like that

growing up gay in the sixties

CAROL E. ANDERSON

She Writes Press, a BookSparks imprint
A Division of SparkPointStudio, LLC.

Copyright © 2017 by Carol E. Anderson

All rights reserved. No part of this publication may be reproduced, distributed, or transmitted in any form or by any means, including photocopying, recording, digital scanning, or other electronic or mechanical methods, without the prior written permission of the publisher, except in the case of brief quotations embodied in critical reviews and certain other noncommercial uses permitted by copyright law. For permission requests, please address She Writes Press.

Published 2017
Printed in the United States of America

Print ISBN: 978-1-63152-314-4
E-ISBN: 978-1-63152-315-1
Library of Congress Control Number: 2017942024

For information, contact:
She Writes Press
1563 Solano Ave #546
Berkeley, CA 94707

Cover design © Julie Metz, Ltd./metzdesign.com
Cover photo © Mauree McKaen
Interior design and typeset by Katherine Lloyd/theDESKonline.com

She Writes Press is a division of SparkPoint Studio, LLC.

Names and identifying characteristics have been changed to protect the privacy of certain individuals.

This book is dedicated to my parents,
who loved me well,

and to Archer H. Christian,
the one whose hand I know belongs in mine.

If you can see your life laid out before you,
that's how you know it's not your life.

—DAVID WHYTE

TABLE OF CONTENTS

PROLOGUE

"Good loves you even if you are a thief, a murderer, or a lesbian," the minister shouted from the TV set in the corner of my motel room. I had stopped channel surfing temporarily when an ad came on and suddenly found myself caught in the clutches of a radical Christian station. I stood up and stared at the preacher, his face red and contorted as he thumped his Bible and blasted me across the airwaves. I'd grown up in a fundamentalist Christian household, and his menacing tone was familiar—piercing. I grabbed the remote, and the screen went black.

I turned to the window and looked outside as I slid my Movado watch over my wrist and locked it in place before returning to the dresser and adding other jewelry: gold earrings, a necklace to match, and my favorite black-and-gold bracelet. Blow-drying my hair, I looked in the mirror as I readied myself to facilitate a workshop for a Fortune 500 company at the Marriott hotel in Atlanta. As I studied my face, I could see the small trace of pain that still remained after all these years of learning to love myself in a society that would place me in the same category with a murderer and a thief. It was the 1980s, and I was in my early thirties.

Voices like that minister's, however faint, remain as haunting whispers even today, thirty years later, as I walk with my partner, Archer, from the parking lot to a performance at the Grand Ole Opry in Nashville, Tennessee. It is raining outside, and I watch the couple in front of us as the man leans down and kisses his date on the forehead, slides his arm around her waist, and pulls her closer to him. They walk in step, smiling. She tosses her blonde curls and looks up at him unabashedly in love, then leans her head into his shoulder with a freedom that I envy.

Archer and I walk behind them. She holds an umbrella in her left hand, and I slip my arm through hers to inch closer. I suspect that most people will assume it is to gain the protection of the umbrella against the pelting water. We look straight ahead, cautious of giving a sign that we are gay in an unfamiliar Southern town. We walk in step also, using the umbrella not as shelter against the rain, but as a shield that conceals the barest hint of intimacy, as I squeeze her arm in a silent acknowledgement of love. The urge to slide my arm around her waist is quelled before the thought is finished, an instinctive response to protect her and myself by keeping the nature of our true connection a secret between us and out of view in this public sphere—even though we are legally married in the United States.

While the law officially protects our right to be together, it does not ensure our social acceptance, nor does it protect us from harassment by random individuals who disagree with the law. The neural pathways laid down in the sixties warn us daily to be alert in public places wherever we are—the impulse is so great we needn't say a word about how we will respond to each other in a new environment. We automatically secrete from others the level of intimacy we share.

This reflexive behavior can engage so readily I don't realize its source until later—like when my partner and I appear at the hotel counter together to check in and are queried by a pock-faced clerk who is probably about twenty, "Are you sure you want a king room? I can put you in a double." Or, when I feel the impulse to let go of Archer's hand when we come upon a group of my MBA students dining at an outdoor café in downtown Ann Arbor, not knowing how my credibility with them might change if they realize I am gay. Or choosing not to reveal to a group of women in the Democratic Republic of the Congo that Archer and I are more than friends committed to a common cause, when they ask the point-blank question "Are either of you married?" Each of these encounters represents a risk I feel in my body; my heart quickens, my hands grow cold, and I divert my eyes, assessing and then deciding with split-second precision the level of threat the inquiring person poses and whether it is prudent to conceal or reveal this part of me.

This shaping began for me in innocent ways—in daily doses at my parents' dinner table, in car rides to softball games, and during Thanksgiving celebrations where I overheard adults in my family speaking in passionate tones about what they really thought about people who were different. Their prejudices slid out past their public Christian personas in ways they didn't see. My mother was worried about the Armenian man who had moved into the house behind us and wore all black. She was afraid he might harm us, though she had no personal contact with him. My Aunt Bet thought we should treat blacks equally but was sure they wanted to live separately from whites. My Uncle Paul was convinced that people on welfare were just lazy and shouldn't be given money that they would only spend on cigarettes and beer. Other messages were shouted at me from the pulpit of the Baptist church, where I endured weekly threats of hell and damnation if I sinned, and on the playground in grade school, where boys screamed "stupid queer" at a smaller kid too frail to defend himself, while I watched him run in the opposite direction, eyes turned toward the ground—the laughter chasing him across the graveled surface. Soon I knew what it meant to be okay or not okay in the family, church, and society in which I lived.

I didn't intentionally absorb these messages. They were burned inside of me like the brand on the side of a steer indicating to whom I belonged and what they expected of me. Without realizing the exact moment my cellular structure was altered by such repeated intrusions into my psyche, I became a prisoner of a way of thinking that demanded allegiance to the tribe into which I was born. I knew what was right and what was wrong, according to the tribal leaders; and if I did wrong, there would be a price to pay. I didn't know exactly what that price was, but I had a sense it would be bad—and if I strayed from what had been declared acceptable, I had to keep it a secret. All too soon, this way of thinking narrowed my ability to hear alternative and greater truths, ones capable of eclipsing those looming large and ominous in the back of my mind and at the front of my heart. Ultimately I shrink-wrapped myself into an alternate version of me—one that my family, church, school, and country would find acceptable.

Growing up in a fundamentalist Baptist household, my robust indoctrination into Christianity began before I could walk. While my parents spoke more often of God's love, our minister focused on God's wrath. And it was his messages that stuck to me like Velcro while my parents' kinder interpretation of the Almighty slid off like Teflon. Both of my parents had a deep faith in their God and called on him to see them through the tragedies they faced individually and together. The most significant of these was the advent of my father's visual disability caused by an incompetent physician, which resulted in the permanent loss of my father's livelihood.

My parents counted on this God to comfort them, to provide

financially when needed, and to bring peace when their troubles threatened to overwhelm them. They also subscribed to a belief in original sin and a future home in heaven if you were saved or in hell if you drifted.

Rereading a letter my mother wrote to me while I was in college in 1968, I see how I was bound by the presumed expectations my parents had of me because of their staunch religious beliefs and how I was lost to the love that flowed so freely behind words that threatened my sense of safety. The religious paradigm, so embedded in her character, made it impossible for me to even imagine, in my twenties, that I could have told her that I was gay. At that age, I couldn't even tell myself.

Today, I hear her voice and see her face—the soft tone of understanding laced with wit, her flashing blue eyes, her half smile—and I imagine her finely shaped fingers typing away on her IBM Selectric while on a work break, thinking of me. I want to reach through the paper and feel the hands that wrote these words, to know in a new way the woman who loved me with a fierce tenderness and a fear that either I was too much or she not enough.

As I read her letter now, I am touched by her words, and I see the broader message she tried to convey; I see how I got stuck on a single sentence that blocked my ability to hear the rest. It was written when I returned to school my senior year in college after a summer home trying to hide my confusion and sadness over losing a woman with whom I had fallen in love. My mother assumed, no doubt, that my unhappiness was about trouble with my boyfriend, Mike.

> *Dear Carol,*
>
> *It was good to hear from you yesterday; I needed to talk to you and find out all was well . . . Sometimes I think when we are together we just talk surface talk, never*

*get inside and know something about how the other one
thinks. Wouldn't it be wonderful if we just decided to open
up our hearts and express the doubts, concerns, as well as
current happenings?*

*. . . We wish we could take some of the sting out of the
experiences for you, but this isn't possible. And through it
all, you have been certain of God's love for you and know
that your times are in His hands. We love you with our
whole hearts, and want to be your best friends . . .*

Take care and always look up!

Love, Mom and Dad

When I received it, I could not let all of her words land sol-idly inside of me. Right there near the end of it was my dilemma: "And through it all, you have been certain of God's love for you and know that your times are in His hands."

I had no such knowing, and, if my times were in God's hands, I was in serious trouble. How could I tell my mother I was miserable, afraid, and in love with a woman—that people thought I was gay? How could I tell someone so sure I was in God's hands when I hoped God didn't really know what I was up to? The letter was not unlike others I had received in my four years at school, filled with references to God, His blessings, and His saving grace. While my mother believed in that God, I was terrified of Him.

Now, I hear great love in her words, her longing to be connected, to ease my pain. As a mother, her intuition told her I was not okay, and she wanted to understand, to help. It isn't that I didn't believe that; I just didn't think she knew what she was asking for and that her response would be to "fix" rather than embrace me. And the rejection I feared compelled me to create emotional distance from her, an act wholly contrary to my natural instincts.

Besides, my mother had had enough to worry about—raising

two kids, working full-time, making repeated trips to the hospital to manage my father's seizures as they experimented with different drugs to bring his system into balance. Her life was hard already, and I didn't need to add to her concerns by telling her that on top of everything else, she had a daughter who was gay.

I don't really know what she would have done had I summoned the courage to tell her the truth, to trust that the love she expressed was deeper and wider than I imagined, that she could comfort me when I felt so desperately alone. I just knew I couldn't risk it.

This was the beginning of trading my authenticity for acceptance. I committed to dating men and carefully monitored my enthusiasm around the women I found attractive and wished I could pursue. I joined with others in making jokes about lesbians to prove I wasn't one of them. Conversations with others about my life became more shallow and meaningless. I cultivated a strong, confident persona that invited others to share their struggles with me while I hid my own vulnerability. Eventually these actions swept away the possibility of deep authentic connection with many who might have accepted me.

In the late sixties, there was a genuine need for protection. Beyond religion's promise of eternal life in hell were the broader concerns of living in a society where mental health professionals still defined gay persons as mentally ill—where you could be fired from your job or evicted from your apartment if people suspected you were gay. And most disturbingly, you could be physically attacked without certainty the laws against assault and battery would protect you. These genuine fears expanded my imaginary ones, exacerbating my felt need for safety in all aspects of my life. My protective antenna streamed out to my circle of friends, my cadre of work colleagues, and especially into interactions with strangers. Over time, I built an invisible shield between myself and others. My ability to alternate between a public persona consistent with the norms of the culture and a private life consistent with my authentic self became as seamless as donning a winter coat to protect my skin against the chill of harsh weather.

Now, decades later, it occurs to me that the danger of revealing my secret may not have been as great as I imagined, and the cost of keeping it may have been far greater than I could calculate.

chapter 1

just as i am

My parents' radical faith in God persisted through hard financial times and even the illness that befell my father when I was a child—devotion they expressed by attending church services every Sunday morning, every Sunday evening, and, often, prayer meeting on Wednesday night. If you looked up *Baptist fundamentalism* in the dictionary, the definition would probably start with, "Thou shalt not," as it related to any form of physical pleasure, or even the occasional delight in a sideways glance at the beauty of the human form. There was no drinking, no dancing, no smoking, no card playing, and certainly no touching of another person by anyone for any reason other than by accident, maybe in an elevator.

Our pastor, Reverend Mitchell, was in his early fifties, and his snow-white hair (flowing back in waves, parting in the middle like the Red Sea) made him look to my young eyes like God himself in a business suit. He was a handsome man of average stature, with a booming voice that rose to the ceiling, bounced off the rafters, and reverberated down the aisles as he bellowed from behind the solid oak pulpit. His consistent message included three main themes: Christ died for your sins and would be back to reclaim his own; you had a choice between heaven and hell; and you should accept Jesus today to wash your sins away. Each point was hammered home with a force that made me fear God might strike me dead before the service was over. I wondered how it was possible to be in this much trouble just for being born.

This view made it hard to reconcile stories of a loving God with someone who would have you burn in hell just because you snuck out of the house to see *Bambi* at the Atlas Theater with the neighbor kids or put a blotch of ink on the back of Annie Stanel's sweater when you sat behind her in fourth grade. I remember my nervousness when I went home that night after the sweater blotch, fearful that God would call the principal himself, resulting in my banishment from Coolidge Elementary School forever. In the Baptist church, it seemed that every unfortunate thing that happened to you was linked to sin—my father's illness, losing my favorite ring, coming in second in the Bible School poster contest. Anything that didn't work out the way I had hoped was most likely due to a moral failing on my part.

Those damning images seared their way into me and became a part of my religious DNA.

Reverend Mitchell ended every service by imploring people to repent. "Now is the time to accept Jesus," he would say softly as the organ music played "Just as I Am" in the background. I hated this part; staring at my best patent leather shoes, my toes tapping impatiently inside my best Sunday footwear, I wanted to dart down the aisle in the opposite direction and bolt from the building.

A hush would come over the congregation, and heads would bow as the music director led us in this closing hymn—a final entreaty for lost souls to come to Jesus. "Who wants to be saved today?"

Once in a while a couple of people would make their way to the front of the church.

"Yes, yes," the reverend would say, raising his Bible in his right hand and greeting the sinner, then putting his left arm around him.

I wanted to be saved. Saved from the endless threat of punishment and a life of fear and anxiety.

As I entered fifth grade, I considered the Catholic religion. They seemed to have more personal freedom around things like smoking, drinking, and dancing. But they had the nuns to contend with, who were pretty scary themselves.

My friend Michelle Davies went to Our Lady Gate of Heaven parochial school, and she asked me to come with her one Saturday to help Sister Mary Martha Caprice catch up on her paperwork. I was elated, and I dressed up in my favorite red Scottish plaid skirt with the oversize decorative gold pin, my cream-colored sweater, and my black-and-white saddle oxfords. I felt bad that they were scuffed on the toes and that the laces were dirty, and I tried to shine them by spitting on my fingers and rubbing the toes while riding in the back seat on the way to the school. My efforts only made things worse, leaving just dark wet spots behind.

Sister Mary Martha Caprice swung open the large-paneled cherry door and greeted us. She wore a black habit with a stiffly starched white cloth that framed her face and squished all the extra flesh toward the center of her forehead, making her wince, even when she smiled.

She welcomed Michelle and her dad and asked if I was there to help too. Suddenly I had the urge to flee across the graveled playground and down the grassy slope onto the sidewalk and fly the eight blocks back home to my own frightening God. But before I could act on that fleeting thought, I was encircled by the long arm draped in black and guided down the hall with Michelle in silence. The floors glistened, and thin slivers of light streamed in through high windows and bounced off of the linoleum, casting long shadows as Sister Mary Martha Caprice floated down the hall in her costume of black and white—two small figures scurrying behind her. I glanced at my shoes with dried spit on the toes and hoped that Sister Mary Martha Caprice wouldn't notice. The whole time I was there I was worried she would ask me if I was Catholic or make me say a Hail Mary if I didn't do things correctly. I didn't really know what a Hail Mary was, except Michelle said they had to say it in school sometimes when they were bad. Jesus was hanging on a cross in every room, flesh pierced with nails and red paint dripping down his side. I wondered if they didn't know he had risen from the dead, but I wasn't about to ask. I couldn't wait to get out of there and was glad when our work was finished and we glided back down the darkened hallway through the ominous black gate out into the sunshine. Becoming a Catholic didn't appeal to me either.

Reverend Mitchell's Sunday condemnations were intermixed with daily thoughtful messages from my parents, whose passionate belief in God helped them see practical miracles in regular life. For instance, they would give generously to the church by tithing but would never ask for help from others. Instead, they would pray—especially when my father made repeated trips to the hospital with unexpected seizures. Insurance always fell short of covering the bills, and he could not be released without full payment.

On one occasion my mother needed more than two hundred dollars to get him out. She relied on God to provide and didn't tell a soul. A few days later, an envelope arrived from a friend with a heartfelt message and a hundred-dollar check. Then one of the men from the steel mill where my dad had been a supervisor showed up at the door with a large piece of butcher paper folded like an oversize envelope. In it, along with messages of hope for my father, was a stack of bills that added up to $127. This was proof for them that God was real and that he was listening. I wasn't so sure, but I thought I had better get myself saved just in case. My brother, Jim, who was two years older, had already accepted Christ and been baptized; so if we all died in a car crash on the way home, I would end up in hell by myself while they all floated off to heaven. With that thought as motivation, I marched myself down to the front of the church during one of those agonizing closing ceremonies and accepted Jesus Christ as my personal savior. I was twelve years old and I was fine, mostly, until I developed my first crush.

I first noticed Gina in the hall at school when I was fifteen. She was hard to miss at five foot ten with her blond ponytail; crisp, white short-sleeved shirts with the collar turned up; and spotless white tennis shoes. The sweet smell of Jean Naté perfume floated behind her and made me want to follow the scent. I introduced myself at O'Shea Park, where we both were wandering around with softball gloves, hoping the boys would let us play. It was the summer of 1963, and for the first time the director of the recreation center announced they would sponsor an official girls' softball team. Gina played first base and could stretch halfway to second to catch a wild throw from the shortstop or race far outside the foul line to grab a ball on the fly. She made me look good at third base, snatching balls in the dirt or ones that flew far above her head. We quickly became a twosome and hung out much of that summer and the next. Most days I would walk down to the park in the late morning and meet Gina. Our ritual was to wear sleeveless shirts and Bermuda shorts, slather ourselves with baby oil laced with iodine, and lie out on picnic tables to tan for a couple of hours before going down to the recreation center to play a few rounds of handball until softball practice at 5:00 p.m.

Lying side by side, the sun beating down on our skin, we talked about high schoolers we knew, about plans after graduation. She wanted to get a job and buy a Corvette. I said I did too, hoping she'd think I was cool like her. Something about being with Gina was special. I'd always had friends, but she seemed different—older, worldly, which wasn't *that* surprising given my sheltered existence. Being around her gave me feelings I didn't have with anyone else, feelings that made my stomach flutter and that sometimes made me feel self-conscious.

Gina was raised a Catholic, and where my mother was Doris Day, Gina's was a Mae West who smoked, drank, played cards, and even went dancing. She had dyed blond hair that she wore pulled tightly back in a French twist, revealing deep lines on her forehead that she filled with pancake makeup. Large oval clip-on earrings framed her face and made her look like a walking cameo. Bright red lipstick accentuated her mouth, and she wore flamboyant colors that surely got her the attention she was seeking. She also wore stiletto heels with straps that crisscrossed her feet—shoes I could never imagine my own mother wearing. Her hands, though thick and rough from her hard days' work, sported polished nails in shades that matched her lipstick. Gina's dad didn't seem to mind her going out with girlfriends. He was bald, stout, and handy with tools—an introvert who seemed to find greater joy in fixing the gutters on the house or trading out the storm windows for screens in the summer than going barhopping with his wife and her pals in their black 1960 Plymouth Fury that resembled a Batmobile.

Gina went to church occasionally and to confession when she felt like it. It seemed that if you could already drink, dance, smoke, and play cards, there weren't many sins left to confess. Religion was not a big part of Gina's life, but having fun was. One day when we were out at the park, she casually pulled out a pack of unfiltered Pall Mall cigarettes and offered me one. I had no idea how to smoke and wasn't quite sure what type of punishment God would mete out for taking a few puffs, but it was the most exciting moment of my adolescence, and I wasn't about to miss it. She carefully unwrapped the cellophane around the package and unfolded the foil on top. Then she slapped the pack against the edge of the picnic table until a couple of cigarettes jutted out. She offered me one first. I pulled one out of the pack; then she took one and provided instructions.

"Put it between your teeth like this," she demonstrated. "Then, when I light it, suck in on the end of the cigarette." Gina lit the match and pulled it up next to the cigarette while she cupped her hands around the tip to keep the match from blowing out. Then she inhaled and effortlessly blew a thin stream of smoke out of her mouth as though she had been smoking all her life.

I sat on the edge of the picnic table and crossed my legs, trying to look sophisticated. I followed her directions, first watching her, then trying it myself. I failed to notice she had inhaled lightly, and when it was my turn, I sucked on it like it was a straw bringing me the last few drops of a delicious milk shake.

As I gasped for air I acted like I enjoyed this new activity though my throat stung all the way to my navel. I secretly hoped this was not going to be a regular part of our ritual, as I was sure it would kill me. I asked if she smoked all the time, and she confessed she had stolen this pack from her mom's carton, assuring me they wouldn't be missed. I couldn't imagine stealing from my mother. I was pretty sure she would know and that there wouldn't be a happy ending to that story.

Gina handed me another cigarette, and in spite of my fear that I would choke to death, I lit up again, struggling less this time, but surely not enjoying it. Thankfully we stopped after a couple, and she promised to save them for the next day.

On another occasion, she talked the maintenance guy at the recreation center into doing her a favor. I was stunned when Stanley waved us over to the tool shed at the back of the parking lot one day and invited us into the musty tin building. Stanley was a soft-spoken black man with graying hair and sweet eyes. He was always friendly and nice to the teenagers who hung out at the center, unlike the gruff older white guy, Ralph. Most neighborhoods in Detroit were segregated, and Stanley was the only black man I had met at that point in my life.

He glanced both ways to make sure no one was watching, then hurried us inside. It was clear he wanted us to hustle, and we obliged. Quickly he closed the door behind us.

The room was lit by the power of a single overhead light bulb that dangled in the center of the shed. He searched for something under the workbench as we stood looking at each other. When he rose and turned toward us, we saw he had a six-pack of Budweiser beer in his hands. I'm sure my wide-eyed expression revealed my shock, though I tried to contain my disbelief. I loved the racy feeling of doing something out of bounds, despite my concern that the cops would burst into the shack and arrest us. For a moment, an image of Reverend Mitchell flashed before me, his wavy hair curling away from the sides of his face, his brow furrowed. I pushed him from my mind before he could speak and concentrated on the scene before me.

There was no room to sit down, so we stood leaning against

the workbench. Stanley pulled out a bottle opener, popped the tops, and handed each of us a brew. So unschooled in the truth about alcohol, while being completely indoctrinated into its dangers, I had no idea how much you had to drink to get drunk. I took one sip and waited. The stuff tasted awful, but I swallowed instead of following my urge to spit it out. The way the Baptists talked, surely a small bit of this potent juice would send me reeling. Nothing happened. So I just kept going forward, taking another sip and then waiting—still no effect. Three sips, four sips—still nothing. I wondered what the big deal was. This was like drinking water. Except water tasted much better. Maybe the effects would take hold later, I thought, so I had better not overdo it.

Gina bragged about how she liked different kinds of beer as I listened, shocked she had drunk *any* beer before, let alone enough to know the difference between one and another. I said nothing, not wanting to expose my lack of knowledge on the matter. I just leaned against the workbench and held the bottle to my lips long enough to appear that I was taking a big swig, when I was just sipping a little. Stanley sat his beer on the workbench and pulled out a pack of Lucky Strike cigarettes from his shirt pocket, unwrapping the cellophane and ripping open the end of the pack. With one good slap against his hand, a few popped out. He took one, lit up, and then offered the pack to us.

Gina reached over casually and took one, put it between her lips, and leaned toward Stanley, who held a match to light it. I didn't really want one but didn't want to be left out, so I reached for one too, put it between my lips, and waited for Stanley to light it, trying to remember not to suck on it like a straw, but to inhale gently.

I kept sipping my drink and taking a few puffs. I was beginning to learn how *not* to inhale, and it became easier to look cool without seriously harming myself. By the time we left, I had probably finished a third of a bottle of beer; Stanley no doubt ended up drinking the rest of the six-pack himself. I was not remotely aware of the incredible risk Stanley was taking—buying beer for two underage white girls and drinking it with them, the three of us alone in a toolshed in the middle of the afternoon in the 1960s.

I made sure no one was in the living room as I slipped through the front door and back to my bedroom, where I took off all my smoke-filled clothes and put on fresh shorts and a clean shirt. I could feel my face turn red as my dad rounded the corner in the hallway, all the guilt racing from my heart up to my head in flashes. I went directly to the bathroom and brushed my teeth three times before my mother got home and then washed my arms and legs with soap and a washcloth. In spite of the anxiety they created, I reveled in the secrets Gina and I shared. Hanging out with her was like flying on the wing of an airplane.

Our friendship grew, and we spent most weekends together—often overnight at her house in her double bed upstairs. We talked and giggled for hours, then would fall asleep in a heap. I would roll over in one direction and she in the other. One night, after I rolled over, I felt her roll over toward me then slide up behind me and slip her arm around my waist in a spoon position, placing her hand beneath my pajama top directly on the bare skin of my stomach. I could feel the weight of each individual finger, electrodes on my torso—soft, light, pulsating. I slid back ever so gently and felt the shape of her body curl around me—the thin cloth of our pajamas the only barrier between skin on skin. I felt an ache that started between my legs and rolled like a tidal wave up my body. Everything was on fire, vibrating like banjo strings about to spring free.

I thought I would burn up the sheets I was so hot, and yet

at the same time I felt frozen in place. I wanted to rise up and swing over on top of her and feel the full weight of my body sink into hers. I wanted to nestle my face into her neck and inhale her smell. I wanted to put my hands on her bare skin and stroke it. I wanted to wrestle with her, dissipate the fireworks that flashed through my body. Should I lie still? Should I roll over? Should I act like I knew what I was doing? Should I act like nothing was happening? What if this was an accident and she didn't mean to put her arm around me? What if she didn't feel the same things I felt? What if God could see this too?

I lay as still as I could, feeling her stomach tight against my backside. Terror and ecstasy in alternating waves rolled on. No one said a word. We just absorbed all that energy in the stillness, as it vibrated between us. If smoking and drinking were sins, I couldn't quite grasp what this might be called. Yet, in the darkness, I could cherish the flesh and deny the guilt. In the darkness, I could push God and the Baptist church far from my mind—aided by the visceral thrill of sensuality.

Her arm was still wrapped around me when I awoke. Light was coming through the window, and I could hear Gina breathing behind me. As the light grew in the room, I felt her arm slip away as she rolled back in the other direction. The magic was gone, replaced by a dull ache that went from the middle of my chest to my belly. The rush and joy of sensual discovery was replaced with the harsh invasion of shame. I felt hot again, but not with pleasure, with disdain. My face was flushed, and I was afraid to look at Gina. I kept asking myself, What are you doing? Gina was cheerful when she became fully awake, and she popped up and asked what I wanted for breakfast.

I thought immediately I should have become a Catholic like her. She didn't seem to have any problem with anything we had done. In truth, we hadn't *done* anything. Yet, something surely had *done* me. I opted for cereal—she nodded and then bounced down the stairs. I lay in the bed a few more minutes, trying to calm myself. After breakfast, we agreed we would meet at the park on Monday. Walking home that day, I felt as though a neon sign was flashing "Sinner" over my head, signaling to everyone on the street what Gina had done and how good it had felt to me. I resolved to never let that happen again. No. Never.

The next Monday at school, when in the library, I went up to the giant dictionary that stood open on a pedestal near the center of the room and, after making sure no one was looking, fingered through the tissue-thin pages until I found the world *lesbian*. It made me nervous to read the definition; I was certain I didn't want to be one.

Yet I was drawn to Gina and would dream about our time together when we were apart, replaying the scene in my mind over and over when I was in my own bed at home. Sometimes I would lie very still and rest my own hand lightly on my stomach, pretending it was hers. Each time we were together, I yearned for the slip of her arm over my waist and the feel of her stomach up next to me, her fingertips on my naked skin. And though I repeatedly promised myself I would never let it happen again, it did—every time we spent the night together. It never went beyond the touch of her hand on the bare skin of my stomach, and the part of me that loved that sensation won out over my anxiety that even that innocent gesture was a terrible sin for which I would pay dearly.

Gina and I never talked about our physical connection, and it remained a secret even between us. In spite of my mother's hope that some boy, any boy, would ask me on a date, the undisclosed fact remained that I was in love with a girl.

⇥⇤

The only mention of sex in the Baptist church was the story of Sodom and Gomorrah and how God punished their citizens for lying together and enjoying the pleasures of the flesh. At the time I didn't know that "lying together" was code for having sex, nor was it clear to me that the Sodom and Gomorrah scene actually involved men being with men.

While my parents were very affectionate with each other, no one talked about sex at home. The closest we came to discussing human biology was when my Girl Scout troop showed the film *When Molly Grows Up*, and my mother took off work so we could watch it together with all the other girls and moms. It was the story of how Molly got her monthly period and how we shouldn't worry if we started bleeding unexpectedly one day.

That was far from a comforting thought. In fact it was scary, as no meaningful conversation followed the film. So I was on my own to connect *my* bleeding with boys, sex, and pregnancy. Given this information, the long-sought-after goal of growing up was rapidly losing its appeal.

My mother made her most serious attempt at a deeper conversation about sex when I was fifteen. She cautiously came into my room one evening and sat tentatively on my bed, where I was reading—on the edge as though ready to catapult herself away if need be. Without warming up to the subject, she just blurted out, "I think we should talk about the birds and the bees."

I wasn't sure if she meant the sparrows and yellow jackets outside or if this was code for something else. It soon became evident. The conversation went something like this:

"Well, you know, love is a wonderful thing, and when you find someone you really care about, then—well—you know—physical things can be very nice."

As she spoke, I noticed red blotches start to appear on her neck, creeping up from her chin to her cheeks and finally her forehead until her entire face was scarlet. I wondered what sort of physical things she meant. Up to this point, I was afraid dancing might get me pregnant. Despite her obvious discomfort, she continued talking, staring not at me, but rather at the purple-and-white pattern on my bedspread, tracing the spirals on the cloth with her forefinger.

"Don't ever let a boy touch you," she said. "He won't respect you after that." She glanced at me quickly and then returned her focus to the bedspread. "Your dad and I waited until we were married, and that made it all the more special." She didn't say exactly what they waited for, but by this time, I was getting the general idea, and my teenage cruelty was somewhat enjoying the sight of her struggle.

She did acknowledge that she and my father had "felt the same exciting feelings that love brings," and that "sometimes it's hard to say no, but . . ."

She didn't finish her thought, leaving me to fill in the blank. She stopped her imaginary drawing on the bed with a pleading look, as if to say, I hope you get what I'm talking about. A slight smile crossed her face, and she looked relieved that she had made it through her presentation. Then she asked if I had any questions.

I smiled back, and though I had plenty of questions, I thought it would be easier to figure out the answers myself than to watch her endure this torture; my pleasure in seeing my usually adept mother fidget like a shy teenager was wearing off. She left me with the overall impression that I should stay away from all physical contact with boys until I was married, that no one would respect me if I didn't, and that good Christian ladies just didn't do things "like that," though "like that" was never explicitly defined. It never occurred to her that she should be warning me about these outrageous feelings with girls.

chapter 2

the diet

loved my mother as well as liked her, and I didn't know how to navigate the tension that began to weave its way into our relationship as I made my way through adolescence, still keeping my secret about Gina.

My mother didn't (couldn't) understand what was going on in my emotional world and seemed intent on lovingly trying to improve what she observed on the outside. Among her concerns was a desire that I act more like a lady and less like a tomboy. She would have liked it better if, as a youngster, I had treasured the exquisite new doll she bought me for my birthday, complete with hand-sewn wardrobe, rather than her finding blond ringlets of its hair in the bathroom sink after I had administered an impromptu cut. Or that I asked for a new skirt for my birthday rather than a saber saw. Probably most pressing was her desire for me to lose weight and take up her penchant for dressing well.

One day, while I was getting ready for softball practice, she followed me into my bedroom. "Remember my friend Joe Greenbaum? Well, I ran into him today, and he had lost fifty pounds."

This was not a conversation I really wanted to have. Knowing I was overweight was embarrassing enough, and I didn't want to hear her recount success stories of old, previously fat friends of hers. I buried myself in my closet, scrounging for my softball cleats. "So I was thinking that maybe you and I would like to go on a diet together," she went on. I kept rummaging deeper into the tangled mess of shoes, hoping she would get a clue and disappear. "Well, what do you think?

Now I was stuck. I couldn't stay in the closet forever. Go on a diet with my mother? I would rather eat carpet tacks. While I had noticed a few more love handles rolling over the waist of her rose-colored Butte Knit dress, she didn't need to lose too much; but she was also smart enough to know that if we did it together, I would have a better chance of success.

"Would you be willing to give it a try?" Having found my cleats, I was now just hiding, my hair brushing against the bottom of my hanging skirts. My face grew hot with a mix of shame and annoyance. The only thing worse than being overweight was your mother talking about it.

"I don't know," I mumbled as I exited the closet. "What would I have to do?"

"How about I just make an appointment and we will see?" I didn't want to say yes, but I didn't want to say no either, so I just got up and nodded as I walked past her, the click, click, click of my rubber cleats hitting the wooden floor.

Without hesitating, she made an appointment for the following week. The closer the time came, the more I wanted to back out. I headed to Gina's after school the day we were scheduled to go, hoping my mother would forget about it. As we played catch in the street in front of her house, I saw the big brown Fairlane 500 turn off of Capital and head down Abington. It stopped in front of us.

I walked over to the passenger's side and leaned into the window.

"Hi, Mom," I said, pretending I didn't know why she was here. She looked at me with one raised eyebrow, letting me know she was serious when she spoke.

"Carol, you know we have an appointment with the diet doctor at six o'clock."

"I forgot," I said, looking away and twisting the toe of my tennis shoe into the pavement. "You know, I don't think I want to go," I continued. "It probably won't make any difference, so why bother?"

I was stalling now and could feel ripples of ambivalence run through me like streamers tied to the back of a bicycle. A part of me did want to go and see if I could change the way I looked. Another part of me was afraid to go through the anticipated embarrassment of it all.

"Well, I'll have to pay for it whether you go or not," she said, staring at me and waiting for an answer.

I wasn't sure if this was true, but knowing that my parents were always riding on the rim of financial desperation, her comment about having to pay struck the intended chord, and I gave in.

"Oh, all right, I'll go," I said, and I got into the car. "See you tomorrow, Gina," I shouted over my shoulder out the window as I slumped down in the front seat and stared ahead.

As we drove along in silence, I thought back to the time when I was ten and my mother had heard about some diet specialist downtown. I had been overweight since kindergarten, and my parents had been concerned. My dad took me in a cab, and we sat in a musty waiting room that smelled like a used-furniture store. The creaky chairs were filled with really fat people—a lot bigger than I was. Eventually a nurse took me behind a curtain and made me take off all my clothes and get on a big scale. I could feel the shame rush through my body from my toes up my legs to my torso, flaring out in blotches on my neck, as I watched the black dial on the scale go up, up, up until it hit seventy-four pounds. My best friend, Michelle Davenport, probably weighed just fifty. I remember thinking that if I didn't eat for two years, I could maybe be the right size when I turned twelve.

This diet doctor was thirty minutes across town—and each ride started with the same inquiry: "How was your day, honey?"

When I was young and we rode in the car together, my mother would make up names for us—she was Mrs. Roosevelt, and I was Mrs. McGillicuddy, personas that allowed us to express any opinion we wanted about anything because we were in a role.

"How was your day, Mrs. McGillicuddy?" she would ask in earnest as she glanced at me while pulling up to a stop sign.

"It was awful, Mrs. Roosevelt. The cat got out and ran for six blocks, and I had to chase him," I would say in my most animated and dramatic way. "He hurt his front paw, and I took him to the vet and had to leave him there. Can we stop for ice cream, Mrs. Roosevelt? I'm really hungry."

And my mother would pull into the Dairy Queen and get us both a cone dipped in chocolate.

I remembered how she made up stories about Tilly the Termite and read me Highlights magazine every night until she fell asleep from exhaustion in the middle of a story. She often hid my Raggedy Ann doll before leaving for work so I would have to search for her when I got home from school. She once concealed her in the ceiling light in my bedroom, which burned off her red yarn hair and scorched the nape of her neck before I discovered her. We had to rush her to the urgent care facility in the kitchen, where I learned that Mrs. Roosevelt was also a surgeon who then performed a combination skin graft and hair transplant in a double emergency operation.

Today, at age fifteen, I hated her question, "How was your day, honey?" I wanted so much to tell her about these strange and wonderful feelings I had for Gina, how I felt special to her, how she, more than anyone I had ever known, made me feel different. I wanted to spill out all of my emotions, let them rush out of my mouth into the air, past all my defenses, to be gently received and understood by her. I wanted to gush on about how good it felt when Gina put her arm around me when we slept together, how alive and safe I felt in her presence. I wanted to tell her that I thought I was in love and ask her if she had felt that way when she met my dad.

Well, that wasn't going to happen. My mother would have driven me straight to a psychiatrist, not to the diet doctor, and I wouldn't be allowed to see Gina again.

The feelings for Gina intensified my felt need to hide inside of myself—telling partial truths out loud and keeping secrets within—my mother and I both suffering from a loss of meaningful connection, because I didn't trust that her love for me was greater than her allegiance to the Almighty. So, when she asked, "How was your day, honey?" I just said, "Fine."

"How about we stop for a corned beef sandwich at Billie's deli afterward?" she said.

I sat up straighter and knocked off the sulk routine. Billie's was a great restaurant with the most opulent corned beef sandwiches I had ever seen. Maybe this wouldn't be so bad after all. I turned toward her and smiled.

"I doubt that that is in their diet plan, Mrs. Roosevelt, but I like the idea."

"Well, Mrs. McGillicuddy, we just won't tell them," she replied, chuckling as we rolled down the road.

This was 1963, long before weight-loss clinics were on every corner and Weight Watchers was a billion-dollar industry. The bald doctor waiting for us was a little patronizing, but I figured I could put up with it if this actually worked. The worst part was getting on the scale again and watching Nurse Charlotte slide the bar farther and farther to the right as I held my breath and watched it creep up from 120 to 130, 140 150, 155, 158 pounds. At 5 feet 4 inches tall, that was a hefty number, and I jumped off the scale even as she recorded it on her clipboard.

My mother tipped the scale at 145, thirteen pounds lighter than my weight. She seemed less distraught then I was, but both of us were grateful that part was over. We returned to the doctor's office and sat through an overview of the program before he sent us on our way with a packet of instructions and a small envelope of diet pills.

For five months I ate eight hundred calories a day—feeding on two meals of protein and veggies with carrot snacks in-between. In addition to the pills, we received an injection at our weekly visit. It was many years later that I realized the little pills were likely speed, transforming both my mother and me into hyperactive maniacs that made the Energizer Bunny look like he had chronic fatigue syndrome.

At my first weigh-in, one week later, I had lost eight pounds. My shorts were already starting to feel loose, and I was spurred on by my early success. The second week I lost four pounds, and two the next. In the first month alone I had dropped a total of fourteen pounds. I was dizzy with the excitement of finding a slimmer me inside a body I always felt was destined to be fat. My mother cheered me on, happy to see that I was using my stubbornness and will power in service of a positive goal, and we bonded over our shared objective.

Though our conversations were limited to relatively inconsequential things during our weekly drive, there was comfort in splurging on the one good meal a week at Billie's. Once there, though, my mother would persist with what felt like an interrogation.

"Are Gina's parents home when you are over there?"

"Yeah, why?" I asked in an annoyed voice as though I were being accused of something.

"Gina just seems to be a little more worldly. What's her mother like?"

I didn't want to tell her she looked like a close cousin of Mae West, so I just said, "She's nice."

I wondered if these were just innocent questions and my fears were triggered by the knowledge that she wouldn't approve of what we were doing, were she to know, or if she had a hunch that something was going on and was trying to get me to tell her.

When I returned to school in September, I weighed a sleek 115 pounds, forty-three pounds slimmer than when I started my diet. Walking to my history class my first day back, I passed my friend Becky in the hallway and said hello. She walked right by me.

"Hey, Becky," I repeated, walking back toward her. She looked at me and squinted as though she was trying to understand why a total stranger was talking to her.

"It's me, Carol. How was your summer?"

"I can't believe that is you!" she said, staring as though someone had jolted her with a cattle prod. "You're so skinny. You look great. What did you do?" She kept staring like she couldn't believe her eyes and saying, "Wow, wow, wow," as we walked down the hall.

I had had the whole summer to watch my gradual transformation from a hefty-looking, un-stylish fifteen-year old to a slim, attractive young woman, whose internal confidence had also flourished along with her outward appearance.

This experience repeated itself with every person who hadn't seen me all summer, and I could tell by the way their eyes lit up that the new me was a big hit. Suddenly, many people wanted to be my friend. While this newfound sense of celebrity was thrilling, it was also disconcerting. I hadn't fundamentally changed as a person at all. I was still funny, smart, athletic, and curious. Only the outer shell had changed. It was like trading in an old beat-up Corvair for a brand-new Corvette convertible—everyone enamored with the outside, the sparkle of the shell, the way things look.

Boys started asking me out on dates, and I, happy to declare myself normal, eagerly accepted. But I didn't find them interesting; and as I listened to them talk on about their various accomplishments as we drove to a concert or out to dinner, I would daydream about Gina, lying in bed with her, feeling the touch of her hand on my stomach and the shiver that sent through my body.

chapter 3

first broken heart

My devotion to Gina was abruptly altered one Saturday afternoon in June when I went to the sidewalk sale at Wonderland Mall with my friend Mary to shop for a Father's Day gift. It was my first awareness of attraction to a guy. Charlie was tall and tan, with short black hair brushed back in a pompadour. He had mahogany brown eyes and manicured brows that hovered over them. His square jaw suggested wealth and privilege, and I knew right away he usually got what he wanted. His hands were elegant, with long, slender fingers that ended in perfectly clipped nails. He was beauty incarnate; I think even my mother had a crush on him.

He was standing in front of Sears and Roebuck behind a table piled high with shirts. His face was a beautiful shade of brown, with a tinge of burn on his nose that made him look like a model for the Sierra Club. Pretending not to notice him, I kept my eyes fixed on the pile in front of me, sneaking a glance with my peripheral vision. At sixteen years old and fueled by my newfound confidence in being attractive, I enjoyed watching him watch me out of the corner of my eye. Then he moved in my direction, picked up a light pink shirt, and offered it to me. "Perhaps you would like something like this?" he said.

I ignored him and kept on walking, but not too fast.

He asked me what I was looking for, and I wanted to say, "I've been looking for you," but I restrained myself and glanced up as though seeing him for the first time. "Oh, I am looking for a shirt for my dad for Father's Day," I said.

He picked up a few colored shirts and offered them to me in hopes one would catch my eye. Finally, I told him my dad was more traditional and asked for something in white as I looked directly into his eyes for the first time. I felt like a swarm of butterflies were flapping their wings at warp speed inside me. I wanted to know why he created these sensations that I had never had before about a guy, a fact that was a wonderful relief. The smell of his cologne drifted past my nose as he reached across the pile and picked out three slightly different white shirts.

"What size does he wear?" he asked, tripping over the guy next to him to get just the right one.

"I think he is a medium. He's about your size." I stalled as long as I could before selecting one of the shirts he offered.

"Do you need a tie to go with that?" he asked. I hadn't needed one when I started, but I was quite sure I needed one now. He slipped around to the front of the table and took me by the arm. The touch of his fingers on my elbow sent waves of delight through my body, and I worked hard to stay balanced as he guided me to the tie racks on the other side of the table. Studying the selection, he carefully lifted off three ties and presented them for my approval.

I felt the material as he held them out to me and enjoyed the sensation of the silk slipping through my fingers. My hands were not visibly trembling, but I could feel the current of energy run through them as I stopped just short of touching his hand.

I let the tie go and pointed to the one with swirls of red and blue. As we walked to the cash register, I reached into the back pocket of my shorts and pulled out my money. At the same moment, my driver's license, which had been tucked between the bills, fell onto the table. He picked it up and read the major descriptors then looked into my eyes and said, "Carol Elaine, that's a nice name."

"Thank you," I said. "I was named after my mother's best friend, Caroline. My mother didn't like the full version, so she shortened it to Carol, thinking that when I was older and more sophisticated, people could call me Elaine."

"Are you older and more sophisticated now?" he asked, with a smile on his face. For the first time I noticed that, in spite of his bold approach and smashing good looks, he seemed shy as he posed the question.

"Pretty close," I said, blushing. He was refolding the shirt now, slipping it back into the plastic. Then he wrapped tissue paper around it and put it into a paper bag.

"Well, you seem pretty sophisticated to me. Would you like to go out some time?"

I thought, Would I like to go out? Oh my God. With you? Yes. Yes. Yes. Absolutely, I would love to go out with you sometime, any time, how about right now? Fortunately, I managed to say instead, "I'll bet you say that to all the girls," and then I followed that quickly with, "Sure, I would love to go out sometime. When?"

"How about tomorrow?" he said, not missing a beat. He offered me a pen and a torn slip of paper to write down my phone number and address. As I reached across the table to hand it to him, I couldn't stop smiling, giving away my obvious pleasure at his invitation.

"So what's your name?"

"Charles, but my friends call me Charlie."

"Well, Charles—Charlie—I will see you tomorrow."

Mary was standing next to me with her mouth hanging open, and I had to touch her on the back to move her in the direction of the car. "See you tomorrow at five," he said as we walked away. I looked back over my shoulder and shot him a smile.

Charlie pulled up in front of our house on time the next day, wearing a starched yellow short-sleeved shirt and dark brown pants. His tanned arms contrasted beautifully with the light shirt, and his brown loafers had little tassels on them that bounced when he walked. You could tell his clothes came from a more expensive store than Sears by the way they hung perfectly on his body and that, despite his forty-minute car ride to my house, his pants didn't show a single wrinkle. I met him at the door and asked him in. My parents, trying not to be overly intrusive, joined me in the living room. After the obligatory ten-minute interview, we moved to the doorway, and, upon his promise to bring me home by 9:00 p.m., my parents released me to his care.

Just sitting next to him on the bench seat of his Chevrolet was a thrill, and it didn't matter where we went or what we did. We spent every weekend together for the rest of the summer until he returned to school at Central Michigan University in September. He was a junior in college, while I was soon to be a senior in high school. Even then, I wondered why he would want to date me, but I didn't care. I was attracted to a guy, and not just any guy—a guy that other girls would dream of dating.

Even after just our first date, those same tantalizing feelings I had for Gina began to surface about him instead. Lying in my bed at night, I imagined his arm sliding around my waist instead of hers. Instead of waiting for her to call or write me a note, I waited for Charlie to call and to write me letters. Instead of feeling anxiety and fear that I was sick in some way, I felt joy and delight in my connection to him. This discovery of feelings for a guy made me overjoyed and reinforced my belief that I must be okay. This new development allowed me to reframe my experience with Gina as nothing more than an immature, adolescent crush on a girl that was of no consequence.

After he returned to school at the end of August, he sent me typewritten letters with SWAK (Sealed With a Kiss) written on the back of the envelope and the Tau Kappa Epsilon fraternity house as the return address. I would read his letters over and over and run my fingers over the typewritten pages as though I could feel traces of the energy in his hands that had touched the same paper.

Charlie's dad was an executive with Seagram's, and they lived in Bloomfield Hills, an upscale neighborhood far beyond our social bracket; but he didn't seem to care that I was working class. Sometimes he would come for Sunday dinner when he was home from school and sit with my family around the table in our tiny kitchen. While I imagined he was more accustomed to a real dining room outfitted with a fine wooden table covered in a linen cloth, sterling silver cutlery, and maybe even crystal drinking glasses, he seemed quite comfortable with our plastic tablecloth, stainless steel flatware, and mismatched water glasses. I was the one who felt uncomfortable.

At the end of our dates, we would park on Capitol, the street that ran perpendicular to Mansfield, where I lived. That way we could make out without my mother coming out of the house and asking what we were doing. Of course, I still heard her verbal messages playing in my head about the dangers of physical attraction, now even more pronounced, since he was a boy and I had no intention of getting pregnant. I loved kissing him, but I wouldn't let him go further than touching me in my clothes. It was too scary to think about messing up my life by doing something that I could never change. If he really loved me, it wouldn't matter that I didn't go all the way. And he wasn't real pushy about it. Back then, few girls had sex with boys outside of marriage, and those who did were referred to as "fast," a connotation that could ruin your reputation.

We continued to date through the fall, and I invited him to my high school football game one weekend, eager to show him off. He happily agreed and suggested I come to visit him at Central sometime. My eyes met his, and I felt myself melt into the bench. Surely, this was what falling in love felt like. And best of all, I could tell he felt that way too, something he confirmed with each new letter he wrote from school.

On November 10, I received his invitation to homecoming. It felt like things were really getting serious when I read his words:

> *Just received your letter . . . GREAT NEWS! Boy, is it ever great that you can come up. It's the best news I have had in a long time . . . Guess what song they are playing right now . . . "Mr. Lonely."*
>
> *I think of you more than anyone else I've ever known— love is the word I'm leaning toward! I'm hurrying with this letter, so forgive my haste. I'm kind of excited too. Waiting for this weekend.*
>
> *Love, Charlie*

There it was in writing: the *L* word. I was riding a wave of delirious pleasure.

Homecoming was fabulous. He arranged for me to stay with some friends of his in a girls' dorm. We went to the football game and the homecoming dance and walked around campus holding hands, and I got my first glimpse of a fraternity house.

In all our time together, we had never discussed religion. I didn't even know what his beliefs were about God, and I didn't care. I had found a boy to love, who loved me.

As Christmas approached, I searched for the perfect present to give him. Cufflinks? A sweater? A monogrammed shirt? Perhaps he would give me his fraternity pin—a sign that this was as serious as I thought. I got him all three. In his letter, he said he would call when he got home for break. It was a week before Christmas, and I still hadn't heard from him. I wondered if he was on a golf trip, since he played on the team and it was too cold for golf in Michigan. Maybe he was finishing finals and had a lot to do. Yet, it seemed strange he hadn't contacted me. My anxiety grew with each passing day. I didn't eat much and couldn't easily sleep. Girls didn't call boys or initiate any kind of contact in those days. Waiting was my only option.

On Christmas Eve the presents sat sparkling under the tree lights, awaiting his arrival to open them. Still there was no word. Throughout the day, when I heard a car turn on to our street, I got up and peeked out the window. I checked the phone repeatedly to make sure it wasn't off the hook, so he wouldn't get a busy signal if he called. I forbade anyone in the house to use the phone except for emergencies. I reread his last letter and searched for clues that something had changed, that I had missed a sign somewhere. While my mother tried to be reassuring, her words of comfort did nothing to ease my worry. Though my father said nothing, I could tell by the look on his face that he wanted to smack Charlie for putting me through this misery. I thought that if he was alive and well and was just letting me suffer like this, I would kill him myself when I saw him.

Christmas Day came and went. Instead of going to the traditional family dinner at my Aunt Jerry's, I stayed home by the phone, certain that he would call me, that he would come. Nothing. Not a call, not a letter, not a word. My parents returned from the family dinner, hopeful there had been some news. They could tell by my dejected state that I knew nothing more. Finally, my parents went to bed. I stayed up glaring at his unopened presents under the tree, the lights bouncing off the shiny red paper I'd wrapped them in. These gifts looked like orphans waiting on a Sunday afternoon for someone to come and claim them. I felt like an orphan, too, as I sat and stared at the tree, watching the tiny pine needles drop one by one onto the unopened packages.

As I sat, his face flashed before me with scenes of walking in the park, his stunning smile that revealed flawless teeth, the warmth of his broad palm in my hand, the smell of Old Spice. I remembered the day we met, his eagerness to sell me a shirt, the way he rummaged through the pile looking for just the right one, that my driver's license fell out of my pocket with my cash, the feel of the silk tie and the way he looked at me. I thought about my trip to Central Michigan University for homecoming, his arms around me like he would never leave my side. Finally around midnight, I got up, went to bed, and buried my face in my pillow, hoping I would sleep for the rest of my life.

On January 2, the tree came down, and I unwrapped the presents myself. Tears splashed on the bright red reflective paper; the gold ribbons, now untied, lay on the rug. Still, I held the hope that maybe he had been in an accident and no one knew to call me. Finally I couldn't stand it anymore and enlisted my pal, Mary, to drive out to Sears with me on the off chance he would be working over his break. I knew he wasn't supposed to return to school until later. We snuck into the men's department, and I hid behind the suits while Mary walked by the belts, the sweaters, and the shirts on sale, directly up to the counter. Since she had been with me when I met him, she knew what he looked like. I saw her spot him next to the case with the watches, cuff-links, and other jewelry for men.

There he was, alive, standing tall and tan and handsome as

ever, wearing his white shirt and red-and-blue tie with the swirl in it. Seeing him in the flesh was like discovering a dead relative was actually still living. Yet I couldn't believe it. If he was alive, why hadn't he called me? Why hadn't he come over? Why had he led me on for months if he didn't mean any of it? My heart felt alternating waves of hope and terror. There must be some explanation for this, but I was too vulnerable to confront him myself. I stayed behind and watched Mary march right up to him and boldly ask, "Are you Charlie?" Her voice was so loud that I could hear her from where I was hiding.

He looked around as though caught by surprise, perhaps wondering if he should admit to his identity. Finally, in a cautious tone, he replied, "Yes, I'm Charlie."

"You know that Carol Anderson waited all Christmas long to hear from you," Mary said, staring intently at him, waiting for an answer. He dropped his eyes from her fierce gaze and stared down at the case of jewelry. I could see that he was uncomfortable. His hand moved back and forth over the top of the glass counter as though he were searching for a message in braille that he could offer to get himself off the hook.

"Well?" Mary said.

Charlie stood still for several minutes, his face flushed. After what seemed like hours, he slowly reached into his pocked and pulled out something and slapped it on the counter as he muttered. I was too far away to see or hear exactly what transpired. Mary stood there, just looking at him, and he nodded toward her and then turned and walked around to the other side of the counter until he was out of sight. My last glimpse of him was through a rack of suits, watching his beautifully sculpted body disappear. My stomach felt like Roto-Rooter had blasted my gut into tiny fragments. I was still trying to gain my composure when Mary said, "Let's get out of here," and headed toward the door, walking with a long stride for such a short girl. I struggled to catch up to her.

"What did he say?" I asked, out of breath. "I couldn't hear. What did he give you?" I wanted to know, and I didn't want to know, at the same time. To know the truth was to give up entirely. There would be no more fantasy reasons for why he wasn't there. It was torture waiting for her to speak.

"He gave me a dime and said, 'Tell her to call me when she grows up.'"

It felt like a verbal knife slashing its way across my chest. I almost expected to see blood pour through my white blouse and my turquoise sweater. What did that mean? Who was this person? He wasn't the same guy I met last summer, not the one who wrote me all those love letters, not the one who missed me and wanted to be with me, not the one that invited me to homecoming or sat in our kitchen and ate my mother's fried chicken.

Mary got in the car and started it up while I sat staring out the windshield. Was this about not sleeping with him? Not letting him have what he wanted? Had he met someone new who would give him that? Did he mind that I was a working-class girl? I could find no answer that made any sense. All of this, and I still didn't know what happened. Too exposed, desperate for his love and affection, I couldn't look at him face-to-face and ask. As we exited the parking lot of the Wonderland Mall, I stared out the window, biting a hole in my lip. I didn't speak all the way home

It was my first realization that falling in love could lead to heartbreak and that there was no explanation for how feelings that powerful in someone could so easily evaporate. I didn't know if I could ever trust someone again, and if I did, it wouldn't be for decades.

chapter
4

the
blood
drive

I t took a long time to get over Charlie. While other guys asked me out, none of them compared to him in any way. They weren't as handsome or as sophisticated. They weren't as mature or as interesting. They weren't as self-assured or romantic. And none of them were nearly as charmed by me as Charlie had been. Most of all, there was no chemistry with any of the others, and my youthful broken heart was certain there never would be.

I started school at Western Michigan University without a boyfriend. Still, it was exciting to be on my own and away from the rigidity of the Baptist church. Though I promised my mother I would find a place to worship in Kalamazoo, I didn't promise I would attend. By my sophomore year, I'd made new friends and eagerly joined many activities—with the exception of the annual blood drive. The thought of being jabbed with a needle made me squeamish, so I usually changed the subject when others suggested we participate. In spite of my skillful efforts to avoid such an outing, I was hijacked one evening by two friends who dared me to come along with them. Easily enticed by a challenge, and not wanting to lose face with my peers, I went, despite my apprehension.

Norma, Carla, and I had just finished filling out the required forms in the union cafeteria, temporarily turned into a frenetic hall full of zealous college students waiting to give blood. Little red stickers with crosses on them adorned multiple surfaces as I glanced around for the exit, hoping no one would miss me if I disappeared. Before I could take action, a tall blond male volunteer came over and smiled at me as he inquired, "Your first time?"

"Yeah. How can you tell?" I asked, looking up into his ruddy face. He smiled more broadly as he replied.

"You look like you are being chased by a cougar, and no one has even touched you yet."

Carla interrupted and introduced me to Mike, a friend of hers, advising me not to let him scare me, as a woman in a light pink apron and nurse's cap escorted her to a table. Mike sat next to me, explaining the process as he handed me a small cup of juice, telling me to drink it so my blood pressure would remain steady and to keep me from getting dizzy or fainting. I gulped it down, and he offered me a second cup.

Great, I thought. This is the best-looking guy I've met in the last two years, and I am either going to pass out or throw up on him. "Do I look like a wuss to you?" I asked, hoping to sound lighthearted as I flexed my arm to demonstrate my strength. He laughed as he reached over and squeezed it with his thumb and forefinger.

As he escorted me to the table where my blood would be drawn, he offered to wait while the nurse set things up. I nodded appreciatively. She asked me to lie down and tightened a piece of rubber around my arm, telling me I had great veins. I took this as a plus. Mike signaled okay with his index finger and thumb and told me he'd be back to check on me.

Out of the corner of my eye, I noticed Carla lying on the table next to me. She turned her head toward me and said, "I think Mike likes you."

"Really, what makes you say that?" I asked, blushing, hoping it was true. He was the first guy I had met since Charlie in whom I had the slightest interest. She went on to say that he didn't pay that kind of attention to most girls, and, in spite of his great looks, he wasn't dating anyone.

Now I wished I had dressed a little better. They'd grabbed me after supper, and I hadn't bothered to fix my hair and was still wearing my jeans and oversize football jersey with a giant number 67. I was asking Carla if he went to school at Western when I noticed him coming back toward me.

"Why don't you ask him yourself?" she said as he walked up.

I felt a flash of embarrassment—not wanting my interest in him revealed prematurely—but went ahead with my question, noting that I hadn't seen him around before. He shared that he lived in town and was a volunteer for the Red Cross. He then walked closer to the table and, looking straight into my eyes with his own robin-egg blues, asked me how I was doing. I nodded that I was fine and noticed the unexpected tinge of excitement his interest brought—something I hadn't experienced in quite a while. Maybe it was his gentleness, or what appeared to be a fundamental goodness, or just the appearance of greater maturity than in all the other guys I had met in college—something made me want to know more. I asked how he was holding up, and he shared that he had been there most of the day and was ready for a break.

A nurse motioned him toward other tables; she needed help with a guy who had passed out. With a smile and a nod, he said, "Need to go. Come find me before you leave."

As I settled into the rhythm of squeezing and relaxing my hand to keep the blood flowing, I closed my eyes, and images of this handsome new guy floated in front of me; I allowed myself to enjoy the pleasure of meeting someone I liked. The flicker I felt was not the white-hot flame that engulfed me when I met Charlie, but a softer sensation, like embers glowing in the dark.

About fifteen minutes later the nurse came back, pulled the needle out of my arm, and asked how I felt. Once I was seated upright, she invited me to stay in that position a little longer before getting down. I scanned the room for Mike but didn't see him; Carla had left a few minutes earlier. Carefully sliding myself off the table, I stood for a minute to make sure I wouldn't collapse and discovered I was fine. Well, that wasn't bad at all, I thought, as I turned toward the exit, looking once more around the room for Mike. I guessed he had left before I was finished. Disappointed, I checked the time and noticed it was 7:00 p.m. Since I needed to study for a test anyway, I picked up my jacket at the door and left the cafeteria.

As I crossed the threshold on my way out, I was surprised to find Carla, Norma, and Mike, all sitting in the makeshift waiting area. Though I tried not to reveal my delight, I couldn't help but smile. "You made it," they said in unison, standing up and cheering and inviting me to join them for pizza. We walked together down the hall, Mike lingering alongside me as I struggled with my jacket; he reached over to help me put it on. Standing next to him, I realized how tall he was and how good it felt to be attracted to someone again. Even if it wasn't like it had been with Charlie, it inspired hope that perhaps I could find another man I wanted and maybe even fall in love.

We went to Bruno's, a favorite spot in town, and ordered two large pizzas with the works. I couldn't believe how hungry I was—not just for the food, but also for the attention of a good-looking guy who seemed to like me. We sat kitty-corner and spent much of the time stealing glances at each other when

Carla or Norma were talking. I noticed how beautiful and soft his eyes were when he spoke and how passionate he was about helping people. He loved basketball, and his eyes lit up when he talked about coaching a group of young kids at the local Catholic school—another nonpaying job. He was at ease with women, not needing to take up all the space with his accomplishments but able to show interest in others. My attraction to him grew over the time we spent together eating and laughing. I hoped he felt the same way.

It seemed that might be the case when at the end of the evening, he walked with us back to the dorm. Carla and Norma, sensing our desire to be alone, went in while Mike and I stood in the lobby immersed in the initial awkwardness that comes when you notice you are drawn to someone and hope they are drawn to you, but neither of you is really sure about the other's feelings. He broke the tension by inviting me out to picnic with him the following weekend.

I noticed his eyes glancing around the room as he posed the question, as though he didn't want to look directly at me, for fear I would say no. While my first glimpse of him at the blood drive showed him confident and unflappable, he now looked reticent. I waited to answer until his eyes met mine and responded with an enthusiastic, "Yes, I would love to."

He moved closer and extended his arms out to hug me goodbye. Leaning into his substantial frame, I felt the wool of his jacket press up against my face. The roughness of it was comforting in a way. He said he would come around 4:00 p.m. on Saturday, and then he asked me for my last name.

Men were not allowed on the dormitory floors, so they had to check in at the desk and ask the receptionist to call up to our rooms to let us know someone was there. I told him my name was Anderson and that I would meet him in the lobby. I waved goodbye, climbed the steps with a newfound buoyancy, and replayed moments of our night together as I closed my eyes to go to sleep.

Mike arrived right on time. He was dressed in a plaid shirt with a button-down collar and light blue seersucker pants with brown penny loafers and no socks. Ever since seeing Charlie's tasseled loafers, I noticed what shoes other men wore. I took much greater care in dressing this time: my best cotton khaki slacks, a white short-sleeved shirt, my favorite lime green windbreaker. As we exited the dorm, Mike headed me toward a large gray truck parked out front. He turned to me and, a bit sheepishly, said, "I couldn't get my dad's car because my brother Steve had it, so we have to take the milk truck."

Within a few seconds I had learned that he still lived at home, didn't have a car, and had some responsibilities delivering milk to customers in our pre-7-Eleven convenience-store world. Inside the truck, the driver's beat-up leather seat was held together with gray duct tape, and an upside-down milk crate served as the passenger's seat. Mike noticed my shock and reassured me it was really quite comfortable once you got the hang of which way to move when the truck turned. The windows were large, and I feared hurtling through one every time I rocked forward, grabbing only at air as I tried to brace myself. Mike gestured toward a metal handle attached to the side of the truck just behind the door, and I grabbed for it just in time on a sudden turn. After repeated starts and stops lurching about, I got the feel of this amusement-park ride minus the seatbelt, track, and safety gear.

We reached Milham Park, and, after finding a spot large enough for the truck, Mike hopped out and went around to the passenger side to let me out. He offered his hand as though he were Lancelot and I were Guinevere dismounting from a horse. Opening the large doors on the back of the truck, he took out a picnic basket the size of a large beer cooler and a huge red-and-black plaid blanket. Inside the basket was the oft-advertised special of Kentucky Fried Chicken, coleslaw, mashed potatoes, and biscuits along with a six-pack of Coca-Cola.

The park was over sixty acres, and we walked past many suitable spots until we reached a favorite of his near the silvery creek that wound its way through the whole park. He spread out the blanket and invited me to sit while he presented the food with a ceremonious flare as though we were dining in an expensive restaurant and he was the waiter. We talked for hours about our lives, our families, and our dreams. At age twenty-one, he was the oldest of eight children; the youngest was three. His father supported the family as a contract milk deliverer for Borden's. His mother took care of the kids and the household. Basketball was Mike's passion, and he dreamed of coaching one day. He was attending the local community college for the time being and was teaching fundamentals of the sport to kids at the local Catholic school. On Saturday afternoons, he refereed basketball games and often took care of his younger siblings so his parents could have a night out.

After eating, we walked around the park and fed the ducks that lingered on either side of the stone bridge, fighting over leftovers that fell from above. Smells of hot dogs and hamburgers sizzling on outdoor grills surrounded us, and a warm breeze rustled the leaves of the oaks and maples as we meandered toward an enormous white pine that captured my attention. With little effort I cajoled Mike into climbing it with me. The limbs were like a staircase, and I easily beat him halfway up the tree before we stopped. I loved climbing trees and had since I was a kid, scaling up the easy ones at O'Shea Park. Trees were one place I could escape from my adolescent worries about being a lesbian and imagine a future where I would be secure in the love of someone, have no financial worries, and be freed from my incessant fears of a punitive God.

As he sat on a hefty branch across from me, staring intently as though trying to figure me out, he seemed to appreciate my athletic ability and spontaneity. I talked about my love of sports, my dislike of dolls, and how challenges made me strive to be better. I entertained him with stories about my softball wounds and field hockey injuries. I shared that my independence had been fostered by a strong mother and a disabled father, who, when I was little, had been robbed of his depth perception and peripheral vision by accidental brain damage. Though I had a brother, we had never been close—each of us dealing with my father's illness in our own way. In fact I had chosen to attend Western Michigan University in Kalamazoo because my brother was enrolled in Kalamazoo College down the road in hopes we might begin to develop a meaningful relationship now that we were both away from home. Mike was one of the few guys I had dated who seemed to really want to know more about me—one who was comfortable asking questions.

"What happened to your dad?

"I was four when my dad got sick," I said as I sat on the limb across from him, my feet swinging back and forth beneath me. "It started with a sore throat. The doctor gave him sulfa, and he had an allergic reaction." He nodded for me to go on. "That night, he started having a seizure and was rushed to the hospital. In order to stop the seizure, they gave him an experimental drug, which put him in a coma."

"That must have been scary." Mike's face showed a degree of compassion I hadn't seen in many men before and that made me feel comfortable sharing more of this story with him.

"Yeah! I was so young; I didn't know what was going on, but I knew I wanted to go with him when they carried him away."

"What did your mom do?"

"Fortunately she had a job as a secretary and spent all of her time going back and forth from work to the hospital."

"Wow, nothing like that ever happened to me." He was clearly stunned by my story and leaned toward me, hands holding firmly on to the branch as he listened attentively to every word.

"He was in a coma for a couple of weeks, and when he came out, he had lost his depth perception and his peripheral vision. As a result, he never worked again."

"Man—how did your family make it?"

"My mom continued to support us, and my dad did as much as he could around the house." I didn't talk much about my dad's illness because I didn't want people to feel sorry for me, but, since he seemed interested, I shared more. "Things like that make you realize that you need to be strong enough to take care of yourself and of others."

I wasn't sure what he would say to that and was relieved when he replied, "I like independence in a girl."

My self-reliance often turned guys off, as men were supposed to be the stronger force in any pairing in the sixties. But this guy seemed to enjoy my self-assured approach to life. I wanted to linger there, take in the scenery from this angle, watch the ducks grabbing for the crumbs that were tossed from the bridge, and enjoy Mike's presence. I was happy. My experience with Charlie, though it ended badly, was reassurance that I was normal. And though I hadn't been attracted to any guys since him, I was relieved that I hadn't been attracted to any girls either. I really hoped Mike and I would go out again.

"Time to go," he said, as the sun started to set. We made our way back down the tree and over to the parking lot where Mike's truck was one of the last vehicles remaining. He held my hand as we walked across the grass, and I felt the roughness of his palm. He was someone who worked for a living, ran the milk route for his dad one day a week, moved crates filled with dairy products, changed the tires on his father's car, and got blisters playing golf with his friends. While he was only slightly older than I, he seemed like he was thirty. Perhaps being the eldest made him seem so mature. It was a quality that made me feel secure. With a flood of siblings flowing behind him, I wondered if he had gotten much of a childhood himself.

The picnic was the first of many dates that spring, and Mike and I became an item, spending much of our free time together. In the evenings, he would come to the dorm, and we would study together in the cafeteria. On weekends we went out with some of his older friends, attending concerts and basketball games.

I encouraged him to finish his classes at the community college and attend Western in the fall to pursue a degree in physical education. He visited me at our home over the summer and charmed my mother completely, bringing her flowers and chocolates. His only failure in her eyes was that he was Catholic—a big problem for Baptists, though no one could explain exactly why. There was no need to worry, however, as we were far from discussing marriage.

chapter 5

over
my
head

Draper Hall was one of the oldest dorms at Western Michigan University. Through my freshman and sophomore years, it was a safe place for me, and in my junior year, I won a coveted position there as a residence hall assistant (RA). Mike knew how badly I wanted the position and sent me a dozen yellow roses when I got the news. I increasingly recognized what a special guy he was—the kind that older ladies would ask to carry their groceries or the Girl Scouts would target for a big purchase. It was clear he derived great pleasure from helping someone in need. On more than one occasion, my mother would say about him, "Now that's a real gentleman, just like your father."

When my mom and I pulled up to the dorm that fall, Mike met us at the car, yanked open the door, leaned in, and gave me a kiss. The smell of English Leather filled the space as I rubbed my hand over the back of his head, appreciating that he'd grown out his blond buzz cut for me. Whether it was acquiescing to my preferred hair style for him, wearing a particular piece of clothing I liked, or forfeiting a night at a basketball game to attend a concert with me, he did it all with a buoyant good nature, eager to make me happy.

"Really, Carol," he said laughing, as he started to unload all my junk stuffed in the car—suitcases, throw rugs, waste-paper baskets, a stereo, table lamps, and racks of hang-up clothes draped in plastic—"Are you sure you brought enough?" He threw his arms around me and held me close. I leaned into him and enjoyed how calming it was to rest my head on his chest. We stood apart and held hands—eyes locked—savoring the moment. This would be the year we found out where things would go.

I ran ahead, got the key to my room, and learned that orientation for the staff would start later that evening. Once I got all the info, I returned to the car, kissed my mother on the cheek, and said a quick goodbye. Mike made repeated trips to my room, taking two boxes at a time up the four flights of stairs. Moving-in day was the only time guys were allowed on the floor. As an RA, I had a simple suite of two rooms: one room for sleeping, the other for studying. The whole space, even the furniture, smelled musty after being closed up for the summer, so I opened both windows and let the fresh air in. I was grateful my mother had helped me shop for bright orange and yellow throw rugs that brought much-needed color to the space.

Setting down the last box, Mike lifted me into the air. "I'm really proud of you," he said.

I was proud, too. Here I was at nineteen, with a fabulous guy, a great new job, and my tuition paid for. My life felt ideal. I started Western in a two-year secretarial course with career aspirations of being a receptionist. All resources for college in my family were focused on my older brother's chance to attend a great school, and it wasn't until the June I was about to graduate from high school that explorations began regarding my options.

I had assumed college was for people like him who came out of the womb reciting their ABC's and knew from elementary school they wanted to be analytical chemists or physics professors.

I had abandoned the secretarial program for a four-year degree as a sophomore so I could join a sorority, and while I still didn't know what I wanted to be, there was more time to figure it out. I was also happy and relieved that Mike and I were getting more serious, leading me to believe marriage could be a possibility if things continued. He was crazy about me and often said so. And it felt especially wonderful that my new job as an RA would provide financial relief. I'd had to pay for college with my summer jobs, since my parents could only provide minor support. This appointment would now leave me some spending money. After he left, I sat down on the couch and imagined sitting with students as they brought me their problems and I dispensed the wisdom acquired over almost two decades of life.

As the new freshmen arrived a few days later, I sat in my room and waited. Bright colored posters with my name and room number hung in the hall so they could easily find me. Soon there was a tentative knock on my door, and a young girl with streaked blond hair and intense blue eyes peeked her head in. Her face was bright with rosy cheeks, and warmth spilled out of her like heat from an old wood stove. I liked her immediately. She introduced herself as Nicky and asked if I could help with her room key. I obliged and tailed her down the hall, taking notice of a cockiness in her step, how her jeans hung loosely on her hips and that her navy V-neck sweater looked like it was borrowed from a much larger person. Rather than shoes, she wore boots with cracked mud around the edges, the laces trailing on the floor as she walked—definitely a girl who wasn't afraid to get dirty. Though she wore no makeup, she was striking without it.

I asked if her sweater belonged to her boyfriend. She replied that it was her father's and that she'd wanted to bring a little bit of him with her. I could understand that and assumed she had a special relationship with her dad, just as I did.

She moved with her eyes toward the floor. Her energy, contained in spite of her swagger, emitted vibrations that were both shy and charismatic. We arrived at her door, and, after several tries, I was able to jiggle the lock enough to open it. Keeping the key, I promised to get her a new one by the end of the day. She thanked me and left the door ajar while she went back downstairs to unpack her parents' car. I continued down the corridor and knocked on doors and introduced myself to the new students. The presence of thirty freshmen filled the floor—the jittery, frenetic energy of young girls feeling the first blush of freedom along with the terror that comes with the absence of boundaries.

After the first couple of weeks, everyone had settled in, and I grew accustomed to my new role, searching for ways to balance my responsibilities with my studies and my social life with Mike. Though most girls on my wing dropped in occasionally, only Nicky came to my room on a regular basis, most often in the evenings after dinner. At first we talked about the more mundane things at school, but soon we engaged in much deeper conversations, asking questions like "What is the purpose of life?" and "Where do we go when we die?" We would continue our dialogues during the day, taking long walks down by the railroad tracks across from North Campus, where we traipsed through the magical landscape of old tin cans, Coke bottles, and bits of trash folded into the weeds and wild flowers that sprouted up through the gravel between the ties.

Nicky would interrupt our conversations as we walked to share the names of different flowers, or stop abruptly to watch a toad or a garter snake peek out from the underbrush. Her ability to spot the movement of the smallest creatures inspired me to take greater notice of things in nature. As a biology major, she loved to explore the natural world; my major in sociology made me love to explore the human mind and emotions. These complementary interests led to conversations about the rights of animals and inquiries into which ones were smarter than people.

She was deeper than anyone I had met up to that point. Her questions were philosophical, her curiosity boundless—her desire to understand the world around her was compelling. Prior to our meeting, I had felt alone in thinking about the things we discussed and was hungry for this kind of conversation. Together, we created a space where we could be more fully ourselves than with anyone else, driven by an innocence and vulnerability that felt precious to me, even then.

One night she began a conversation with the question "What is love?"

I looked up and saw her face in a new way, noticing how beautiful her features were in the low light. I fixed my eyes on her hair, which hung over her right eye, and watched how she tossed her head and ran her fingers through it, pulling it behind her ear. It was a gesture I had seen many times before, but tonight it had a sensual quality. Her eyes were soft, her cheeks flushed. She fixed her gaze on mine, and we lingered longer than usual, neither wanting to look away. When my eyes did drop, I noticed the curve of her fingers as she smoothed the corner of a paper on my desk and how I wanted to take hold of her hand.

"What is love?" I repeated the question. She had a habit of striking matches while we talked and watching them burn. Just then, she lit one and held it in front of her face. We both watched the tiny fire in silence as it crept along the thin wooden stick till she blew it out just before it reached her fingers. It seemed like a metaphor for this moment. Something was on fire here

for sure. Her gaze remained steady, and I imagined she asked
that question for a reason—that it was possibly an invitation to
talk about a feeling that was growing between us. The intensity
enlivened and terrified me. I had thought about that question a
lot before and wrote about love in my journals, but no one had
ever asked me the question, and never a girl who was looking at
me the way she was.

"I think love is a mystery. No one knows where it comes
from, or why it ever leaves. It is more powerful than anything
on earth, and yet we are totally dependent on someone else to
give it to us."

I stopped for a moment, picked up the matches, and struck
one myself. We watched it glow as I went on. "You can't create it
or control it, and, while it is more valuable than anything else,
you can't buy it anywhere. It is given for free, and that is what
makes it rare and precious."

The fire had reached my fingers just as I finished my sentence, and I blew it out. My heart thumped in my chest, a
metronome of warning, telegraphing memories from the past.
Here it was again, this unbounded feeling of flying, this incessant desire to be closer, to fall into this invisible prism of light
and color, to feel the touch of her hand on my skin.

I wondered in silence if she felt the same way—if she could
not only see the flame but feel it. Her hands reached for the
matches, and as she took them from me, I felt the slight brush
of her fingers. It made me quiver. My mind flashed back to the
sensual connection I felt with Gina, and I wondered if Nicky had
had an experience like this before with another woman. The
slow-motion quality of this conversation unfolding, along with
the rush that came with the slightest physical touch, made me
think there was intention behind her question.

"Have you ever been in love?" she asked.

I was afraid I was falling in love at this moment and that she could see it. "Yes, once." I was not ready to admit I had been in love with a girl when I was fifteen, for fear I would scare her and myself. Gina and I had grown apart when she graduated high school half a year before me and got a job as a secretary. Going on to college, I was sure that had been a once-in-a-lifetime young-girl crush that was behind me. But, I could talk about the boy who broke my heart.

I told her about Charlie and how I thought he was someone special who turned out to be kind of a jerk. I reached into my desk drawer and pulled out photos of friends and family back home. I searched through the pile and held out the one picture I had of him.

"He's very handsome," she said, taking a long look at the photo.

"Yes, he was really gorgeous on the outside, but in the end not so much on the inside. In fact, I never really found out what happened. He just disappeared one day." I didn't want to talk about Charlie. I wanted to stay in the feelings I had right now with Nicky. "What about you?" I asked.

"That conversation would require more time," she said, as she yawned and slowly got up from her chair. I came around to the other side of the desk as she reached out her arms to hug me goodnight. For a second I let my face rest next to hers and feel how smooth it was. We stood there for what seemed like ten minutes, though I am sure it was only seconds. It was thrilling leaning in to her body—so closely pressed together I could feel the beat of her heart. Yet, it wasn't just physical; it was an experience of knowing someone better than I had known anyone. I felt like I was holding love itself in my arms, and I didn't want to let go.

I closed the door behind her, leaned back against it, and silently murmured to myself, "Oh my God, not this again." I got into bed and closed my eyes but couldn't sleep—images of Nicky kept appearing, each of us fixated on the match in her fingers burning down, feeling the heat and wondering what was going to happen next.

These feelings of intense attraction were launched, and I couldn't stop them; nor could I quell the anxiety they generated. I had thought I was over this. Charlie had convinced me that I was normal, and my attraction to Mike was reassuring. But this hunger was wild, racing—an out-of-control desire to be right up next to Nicky. No doubt somewhere in our shared unconscious there was a craving to be closer physically in a way that matched our growing feelings of mental and emotional connection. At first we met it through athletic competitions, chasing each other outside and wrestling ourselves to the ground—disguising sexual attraction with physical play.

One night, this contact expanded to a softer version when Nicky offered to give me a massage after I complained of a sore back.

"Come on," she said, as she pushed me toward my bed in the other room. "Lie down. I'm really good at this."

Without resisting, I agreed and carefully took off my shoes and placed them beneath the bed before I lay down on my stomach fully clothed in my corduroy Levis and cable-knit sweater. She sat on the bed next to me, and I could feel her hip lean into mine as she bent over my back and pressed her hands down on my shoulders, releasing the knots. Even through my thick sweater, I could feel both the strength and tenderness of her fingers and the sweetness of her touch.

"Why don't you take this off?" she said, yanking on my top after ten minutes of earnest but fruitless effort. "The knots in your back are really bad, and I can't get at them through your sweater."

Raising myself up, I pulled it off over my head and tossed it on the chair across from the bed. After I was facedown again, Nicky climbed up on top of me and sat on my backside, her legs straddling my body.

"That's better," she said, as she started at the top of my back and lightly pulled her fingertips across the bare skin of my torso till they reached the edge of my belt. Then she leaned forward and gripped my shoulders with both hands and pushed at the knots with her thumbs repeatedly until they softened. She then worked her knuckles into my upper back, kneading the tissue from top to bottom. She repeated this same pattern for about twenty minutes.

"Is it okay if I push into you with my elbows?"

I nodded, uncertain what she meant but willing to find out.

Slowly, she placed the points of her elbows into my shoulders and then gently lowered her body onto mine, her elbows sliding to the sides, until I sensed her full weight pushing into me, felt her breath on my neck and her hair sweep across my shoulders. She was so close that I could smell the freshness of the Irish Spring soap she used. It was like a dream in slow motion as she raised herself up and again smoothed her hands across my back in soft even strokes—our blended energies swirling between us. I wondered if she could feel my pulse racing or the electrical currents that sped down my arms and legs, making me light-headed. Alternating emotions of ecstasy and panic were followed by the profoundly unsettling awareness that I shouldn't be feeling this way.

Silently, I reassured myself that this was okay, that we weren't doing anything wrong—it was just a massage. My musings were interrupted by a loud knock on the door that startled us both. Nicky jumped off of my back as I quickly reached for my sweater and pulled it on over my head.

"Just a minute!" I shouted, fearful that the person would walk right in and wonder what was going on. Smoothing my hair, I went to the door and opened it just enough to peek my head out. "Hi, Betsy," I said. "What do you need?"

"Have you seen Nicky? She was going to help me with my biology homework." Nicky hadn't mentioned anything about it.

"Yeah, sure—as a matter of fact, she's in here." I tried to sound nonchalant as I turned toward the other room and called out, "Hey, Nicky—Betsy's looking for you."

Nicky emerged from my bedroom with a sheepish grin on her face, walked past me, and said, "Want to meet for lunch tomorrow?"

"Sure," I responded, as she joined Betsy in the hall. "Have fun, you guys."

I closed the door and rested my hand on the knob. My heart was still drubbing wildly. I turned out the light in my study and lay back down on my bed with one hand on my chest and the other on my stomach, hoping to calm the surge of wild sensations. The scent of Irish Spring still floated in the room. What did it mean to feel this fierce attraction to her? Was there something wrong with me? Did she feel this way too? I didn't want to dwell on any of it, but the thoughts and feelings were too powerful to ignore. I tossed and turned with them most of the night.

It seemed that we had made another step that night toward greater acknowledgment of the invisible force field surrounding us. And though I was certain both of us felt it, neither of us could speak it. One part of me was grateful Christmas break was a few days away so we would have some time apart to calm the constant rush of feelings that cascaded between us. Another part of me wished that Nicky were coming home with me for the holiday instead of Mike. That thought really scared me, because I knew it should be the other way around.

chapter 6

pain, pleasure and confrontation

While I was home on break, my grades for the first semester of junior year came in the mail. I knew my performance was not going to be outstanding, but I was unprepared for the shock:

Cultural Anthropology: D
Design 1: D
Art Survey 11: D
Art History 1: D
Bowling: A
Teaching and Learning: A
GPA: 1.86

Here in black-and-white were the harsh consequences of all the nights and days spent in conversation with Nicky. Great, I thought. Now, because I didn't get a 2.7 GPA, I would lose my RA job and have to face all of my friends, who would then know I had failed.

I slipped out the back door, through the alley, and down to the park. It was snowing, and large round flakes caught on my eyelids as I wandered across the softball field where Gina and I had played. I found a seat on a picnic table and cleared away the tears with my mittens—the cold snow on my face sent an even bigger chill through my body.

Sitting there, I remembered all the summer days I spent with Gina—sunbathing on the picnic tables, playing softball till the sun went down, smoking cigarettes and trying my first beer. Above all I thought about the sleepovers, where under the covers, she would roll toward me and slide her body up next to mine. I could feel the thrill all over again as I recalled the moment she slipped her arm around me. All of those same feelings were here once more with Nicky—the rush of physical sensations when she gave me the massage, the overpowering desire for her to lean into me, to feel her breath on my neck and the touch of her hands on my skin. I wanted to get out of my body, my head, out of this funnel cloud of fear.

I knew I had brought this on myself with all the time I spent with Nicky, skipping classes and staying up all night talking. Even as I faced my unknown future, I couldn't have given up those precious moments. Worse, I had no one in whom to confide about this tangle of love and fear, guilt and joy, and always the undercurrent of gripping anxiety. It was 1967. There were no gay advocates, no magazines or books I knew to read, and there was nowhere to go to find either—certainly not the minister of my church, not my girlfriends in the neighborhood or at college, and, despite my parents' letters of love and concern, most certainly, not them.

The temperature continued to drop, and I made my way back across the park to home, where I stole away into the bathroom with the phone and dialed Nicky.

"Oh, Andi," she said, using her nickname for me, after I told her about my grades. "I'm so sorry. You must feel awful." Her sincerity melted the barrier I'd built to shield myself from the judgment I imagined would come from everyone who found out. "What are you going to do? You are coming back, aren't you?"

The frantic tone in her voice gave me comfort—she really cared about me.

"At the moment, I just feel like running away."

She suggested that I run to her house, and if she hadn't lived two hundred miles away, I would have—gladly.

I heard my mother's car pull up. "Mom's home. Gotta go," I said, and I abruptly hung up.

My mother was in a good mood as she walked up the steps. Christmas always cheered her, as she loved to buy presents, bake cookies, and have people over. I met her at the door and took the bag of groceries she carried.

"What's the matter, honey?" she asked as soon as she saw my face. My mother had a way of knowing when things weren't right no matter how hard I worked to disguise my feelings. There was no point acting like nothing was wrong, and the sooner I got this over with the better.

"Well, I got my grades today," I said.

"It couldn't be that bad." My mother, the perpetual optimist, had no idea how bad it could be. She was not a big yeller or one to become overly dramatic about things. That would've been easier for me to deal with. The thought of disappointing her was the hardest. Especially when my older brother was a mini UNIVAC computer when it came to school—getting all As from kindergarten through college.

"I got four Ds and two As."

Her eyes got wider as she stifled a gasp, and she looked as though she hoped she hadn't heard me correctly. "Are you sure that's right?" she offered, hopeful that it was a clerical error and not the result of multiple bad decisions on my part.

"Yeah, I'm sure."

She came over and put her arms around me, and I started to cry. All my fears and feelings came racing out through my tears—my secret attraction to Nicky, my ambivalence about Mike, and my anger at myself for ruining a great opportunity. A few moments later, my dad came into the kitchen, stood close to us both, and laid his hand on my shoulder. Even without knowing what had created the scene before him, he was eager to comfort.

"What's the matter, pudding-head duffy?" he asked gently. I hated to admit to them both that I was on the verge of flunking out. I told him of my pathetic performance.

We all just stood there as I felt my father's hand gently stroke my head. After several minutes, we all sat down at the kitchen table. My dad took my hands in his, looked straight into my eyes, and spoke his oft-repeated refrain: "You know, Carol, there will be lots of bumps along the way in life, and it doesn't matter so much what happens to you. It's how you handle what happens to you that makes the difference." There was compassion in his voice. I could feel it streaming through his body out of his arms into my hands—like a transfusion of love and hope. He told me, as he often had throughout my life, that he believed in me with all his heart and was certain I could overcome this. He reminded me that I was smart and creative and capable and, above all, that I had the courage to go on.

My mother chimed in, "It is just a little setback, but it doesn't mean anything about who you are or how much we love you."

I told them I felt mortified and wasn't sure I wanted to go back. They reassured me that I would recover from my embarrassment and that this was an important test of character. I needed to show myself I had what it took to rise above adversity, and they believed I could do it. My parents always showed their greatest kindness to me in my darkest and most vulnerable moments—focusing on the important lesson to learn, rather than condemning my shortcomings.

The first few weeks back at school were awkward. I had to face all the freshmen on my floor and tell them that I wouldn't be their RA anymore, though I'd be around if they wanted to talk. I settled into a downsized single room on the third floor, which sported a set of stacked bunk beds against one wall and a tiny wooden desk against the opposite wall. Both pieces of furniture were scarred with scratches and bits of chipped wood that revealed rough use over many years. Gone was my lavish suite of two rooms and the luxury of space. Gone was the privilege of having an identified leadership role in the dorm. Gone was my sense of pride in having my tuition paid for. These visible losses were a big wake-up call. I was determined to stop fooling around with Nicky and focus on my grades and my relationship with Mike.

While my intentions were clear, my resolve was weak, and I easily succumbed to any adventure Nicky suggested. One Saturday morning she bounded into my room out of breath and said, "What do you say we go downtown and take the next Greyhound bus, wherever it's going?"

I couldn't resist, and, grabbing my coat, we took off down the stairs, buoyed by the prospect of an escapade. We arrived at the bus station, checked out the schedule, and found that a bus was leaving for Benton Harbor in fifteen minutes. We bought our tickets, got on board, and sat near the back. Sitting side by side in the confined space permitted us to lean into each other and enjoy the physical sensations that danced between as we talked and laughed all the way there.

Our intention had been to get off, walk around the place, and then get back on the bus and come home. We were so excited by the adventure that we failed to check the return schedule prior to boarding. Only upon arrival in Benton Harbor did we discover that no buses were going back to Kalamazoo until the next morning. Our choices now were to call Mike to come and get us or spend the night; I had to call him in any case to cancel the date we had for the evening. We looked at each other, shrugged our shoulders, and together said, gleefully, "I guess we have to spend the night."

I looked around for a phone booth in the bus station, dialed Mike, and waited, slightly worried he would be upset by the change in plans. I listened to the ring as I twirled the phone cord around my finger and read the graffiti on inside of the booth. He was generally easygoing and often found my impulsive actions funny or at the very least entertaining when they involved him. Finally, he picked up the receiver.

I tried to sound upbeat, hoping he would see this little trip to nowhere as kind of a lark, that he could appreciate the fun of it all. I began with, "Hi, honey, you'll never guess where I am."

"No—probably not."

"Well—I'm in Benton Harbor with Nicky. You know how I like to be spontaneous . . ."

"What?" he said, annoyed. "We were going to go to the basketball game tonight with Bob and his wife."

I had not heard this tone before; I had crossed a line. I softened my voice in my reply. "I'm really sorry. We didn't realize there wasn't a bus coming back tonight. I know it was a reckless thing to do."

"Carol, I'm really disappointed."

My gut tightened; Mike had never said that to me before, and I had taken him for granted more than once in our relationship.

Now, I felt sheepish. I apologized again and let him know I understood why he would feel that way. My impulsiveness had gotten me in trouble on other fronts in the past, and I knew he was right to be angry.

"What time does the bus get back?"

I told him it was around noon and asked if he would like to have lunch together. It was quiet on the end of the line as I wound my hair around my finger and held my breath, worried he may never want to eat any meal with me again. I implored him not to be angry, though I really couldn't fault him for whatever he felt. I would have had a fit if he had done something like that to me. "I love you," I said tentatively.

"Call me when you get in. I'm not feeling very hungry at the moment."

I sat there for a few minutes. Even I could see how selfish my actions were. Torn between my loyalty to Mike and my attraction to Nicky, I allowed the intensity of my regret to dissipate as I walked away and rejoined her; she was counting her cash to see if we had enough between us to get a hotel. She could tell by the look on my face that things hadn't gone well.

"I think I went a little too far this time," I said, furrowing my brow and running my hands through my hair. "I really hate hurting him. And . . . I love it that you are spontaneous like me." I talked myself into believing things would be all right as I reached into my pockets and pulled out a few bills and some change. Between the two of us, we had a little over forty dollars. Master-Card had barely been invented (and my parents didn't have one), so cash was the only option for payment. We looked at each other and laughed—having no idea how much a room would cost for the night—and set out on foot in the direction of some possibilities.

We walked two blocks and found a small independent motel that looked a little dumpy but was in our price range. We paid our money, went up to the second floor, and opened the door to modest furnishings—one double bed, a small black-and-white RCA TV, and a desk with a lamp and a Bible on it. I opened the window to let in fresh air; then I put the Bible in the drawer.

We had passed a pizza place on the way, so we went back and got a small deep-dish to go and took it back to the room. We spread out one of the threadbare towels on the bed as a dining cloth and then sat cross-legged on either side to share our picnic.

The dim lights intensified the feeling of mystery and anticipation. Whatever it was about Nicky, being around her always heightened my senses. I felt the familiar waves of sexual attraction as I watched her take a bite of pizza and chase the dangling cheese with her fingers, scooping it up and putting it in her mouth.

Around 9:00 p.m. we turned on the TV and lay apart on the bed, still fully clothed; we fell asleep watching *I Love Lucy*. Midway through the night, we climbed under the covers, and, just before drifting off again, Nicky rolled over and slipped her arm around me, just like Gina had years ago, drawing me into her body. The same voltage I experienced back then seared through me, and I savored the sweet torture—to be so close to her yet unable to free myself to feel the full glory of physical connection. While my mind kept saying, "Stop this," my body kept saying, "Get closer, this is what love feels like." I didn't want to go back to sleep. I just wanted to lie there and listen to Nicky breathe and feel her tenderness and her strength surrounding me, knowing that when the morning came, all of this exquisite pleasure would be gone. And, in the light of day, the guilt and self-hatred would rage over me with the force of Niagara Falls, making me despise myself for loving something this beautiful.

Mike forgave me and came over the afternoon we returned. We spent most of the day together wandering around Milham

Park holding hands, tossing bread crumbs to the ducks, and sitting on the bridge beneath the tall pine tree we climbed on our first date. Guilt swarmed inside me as we strolled. He was such a good man in every way—kind, caring, thoughtful, reasonable. Even as I reminded myself of his many superior qualities, my thoughts returned to my time in Benton Harbor—eating pizza on the bed, watching Nicky's face in the reflected light of the television, the way she turned her head and swept the hair out of her eyes, and the evocative feeling of her arm slipping around me as we fell asleep.

While there was a sexual revolution going on in the sixties, it was about greater freedoms for heterosexual men and women to explore sex with multiple partners, inside or outside of marriage, or for women to challenge laws that prohibited them from using birth control. In the absence of any similar public discourse helping same-sex partners understand and joyfully explore their feelings, Nicky and I were alone in our attraction, never talking about it openly—not even to each other.

Then, one night, as I was sprawled out at the foot of my bunk bed in the dorm talking with Nicky, who was on the top bunk, she unexpectedly descended from her perch, turned out the overhead light, and lay down next to me. Inching closer, she curled her body around mine. The feeling was tender and breathtaking, the smell of her hair sweet, as she nuzzled into my neck. It was luxurious—just as it had been the night in Benton Harbor. We lay there in silence for a few minutes before she raised herself up on one arm, bent her head over my ear, and circled the inside of it with her tongue.

My body went limp, and I knew for sure that this was no accident. Gone now was all resolve to deny the intensity of our attraction. She lowered her body on top of me, rested her cheek next to mine, and stroked my hair with her hands. She kissed me on the forehead, then on my cheek, and finally on my lips. It was otherworldly—the softness of her face, the gentleness of her touch, the weight of her body. All night long we lay half awake, half asleep, as we savored the sensation of being pressed up next to each other. While the familiar threats from my Christian upbringing marched in and out of my consciousness (along with glimpses of Mike's face looking aghast), I didn't care. My body was in charge, not my brain, and it had hungered so long for this moment, it was irresistible. As the morning light came in, I brushed her blond hair away from her eyes and touched her face to awaken her. We looked at each other in silence, no longer protected by the darkness of night.

"I really don't want to go to class," she said.

"Neither do I," I responded as we both got out of bed, now feeling shy and self-conscious, glancing at each other with uncertainty about how the other felt. We smiled and hugged before she left, sharing a secret that still had no words. When the door closed behind her, I sat back down on my bunk awash in a jumble of feelings. I wanted to relish the sweetness of this innocent love before the face of Reverend Mitchell or my mother came smashing through my psyche to rip it away. His voice intruded as I got up and got dressed: "The wages of sin is death . . . repent and be saved." I kept moving as I pushed the words outside my head.

Nicky frequently spent the night in my room that spring, and, each time, I felt tormented by the contrast between my excitement over her and what felt like brotherly love for Mike. It was as though I had gotten the signals switched. I could only manage this angst by compartmentalizing my public relationship with Mike, who made me feel normal, and my private love for Nicky, who made me feel whole. It helped that Nicky was a favorite of my mother. But even this delight was confounded by my fear that should my mother ever find out the true nature of our relationship, she wouldn't like her at all. This caused me to once again be extra cautious about what I shared with my mom. It was contrary to both my body and soul to feel such great passion for Nicky in private and to suppress it completely in public. Lying with words is difficult; lying with your body, impossible.

Meanwhile, my relationship with Mike was progressing, at least on the surface. He agreed to attend the Baptist church with me, which further endeared him to my mother. Nicky pledged my sorority. She and I visited each other's homes on the weekends when Mike had other plans, and we double-dated on special occasions. After dropping off our respective dates in the lobby of the dorm, sure to have others notice us leaning against the walls making out with them before they departed, we would retreat to my room, turn out the lights, and climb into bed together. We carried on as though this split-level life could continue forever, never bothering to inquire how long it would be sustainable.

The answer to that question came in the middle of March when Nicky came down with a severe case of mononucleosis and had to go home. A dull emptiness crept into my body from the moment I got the news. Corresponding with that announcement, coincidentally, I was summoned to a meeting with Judy, the assistant director of the residence hall. Nicky was sprawled out on the lower bunk in my room, half asleep as she struggled to do her biology homework, when I left for the consultation.

I suggested she stay there and rest until I returned. It was unlike her to be so low in energy, and it worried me. I left quietly and headed to the director's room. The door was closed, which was unusual, so I knocked and waited. Judy opened the door slowly; all the RAs were sitting in a circle. None of them stood up to greet me, give me a hug, or banter in the way we once had when we all worked together. The dim lighting made the institutional lime-green walls feel even more oppressive than usual. My hands were clammy, my throat dry. My heart pounded so fiercely I feared others could hear it.

"How are you doing?" Judy asked as I took the empty chair in the circle.

"I'm not sure—maybe you could tell me," I said. "Is something wrong?"

I was scared. I had visions of my parents being in a car wreck or my mother having a stroke at work. Surely someone must have died to create the heaviness hanging in the room. Finally, Dottie spoke.

"You know we are your friends . . ." She paused for a moment before continuing. My body stiffened, anticipating a blow. "We just wanted to let you know that people are talking about your relationship with Nicky."

My eyes were fixed on the brown tile as I counted the flecks in it and noticed how the sun had faded the ones closest to the windows. My lip curled inward in an effort to keep back the tears. I knew what was coming next, though I wanted to cover my ears and not let the words reach me.

"They say that you are sleeping together. In fact, people are saying that you're gay."

I stared past the people in the chairs and out the window. Spring was near, and the sun was bright on the trees. People in light jackets walked from the library back toward the dorm, and a couple of girls played catch on the front lawn. I felt my lungs collapse inside my chest, desperate for a deep breath that would sustain me through this nightmarish scene. I didn't know what the punishment would be if the truth were known, but expulsion was the first thing that came to mind. I wouldn't let them make me admit it. I wouldn't allow the truth to harm Nicky or me. I sat still and tried to keep composed though the overriding sensation was one of defeat—trapped in the enemy camp with a sword to my throat. Of course people would think that. Of course they would imagine we were gay. Of course they would make it ugly. It was an indefensible position—most of all because they were right. She did spend the night in my room. We did sleep together. I did love the feeling of her arms around me, the touch of her skin next to mine, the way her hands moved in the dark to pull me closer to her. I loved the sound of her breathing, the way she looked in the morning, her shy tenderness, the way she touched my face when she kissed me.

My ears were hot, and my hands turned to fists in my lap as I prepared to speak. Instead of confirming their accusations, I responded with an incredulous, "What? That's ridiculous!" My gut roiled with the force of this lie, my chest heavy with despair.

Dottie persisted. "Well, is it true?" she asked in a derisive tone.

"She's my best friend. Is there a problem with that?" I tried to convey an appropriate balance of surprise and indignation. "So, who's saying that?" I asked, taking the focus off of me.

"We are not going to name names, but it's more than one person."

I wanted to throw up, run out of there, smash something. Instead, in the calmest voice I could muster, I said, "Sure, we spend time together, but it's no big deal," as though Nicky meant nothing to me.

"Does she spend the night in your room?" Jane asked in a tone that made me feel I was being interrogated by the relationship police.

"Yeah, sometimes—but I have bunk beds, you know. I find this insulting!" My voice strained as I kept denying the allegations.

"Carol, you know we are your friends." Really? None of this felt very friendly. It felt harsh, accusatory, humiliating. I glanced around the room, but no one's eyes met mine. Heads down, staring at the tile, they spoke to the floor as though I weren't there.

Sherry weighed in, "Sometimes people make things up, and, whether they are true or not, they can ruin your reputation." Why would loving someone ruin your reputation? I thought to myself. Tethered to my chair by invisible ropes, eyes cast down, I was unable to speak.

"Are you okay?" Dottie asked. "We just wanted to let you know that we're concerned."

"Yeah, I'm fine," I lied again as I stood up to leave. "Is there anything else?"

"You might not want to give people the wrong impression," Judy said in closing.

But they already had the wrong impression on all counts by making our relationship something to be ashamed of rather than to celebrate, and there was nothing I could do to give them the right impression because somewhere inside I had the wrong impression also.

"Okay then—nice poster," I said as I nodded at the *Planet of the Apes* wall hanging and turned to the door. I reached for the knob and yanked it hard. Out in the hallway, I half expected a crowd of girls to be there, jeering at me. No one was around. I turned left and hurried toward the back stairs. Torrents of shame squeezed my chest like a cider press. God didn't need to punish me. I could do that myself—by lying to people in order to preserve my identity as a straight person, by lying about the one person who meant the most to me.

I raged inside at them, at myself, at Nicky—anything to stop the pain. I was going against everything my parents had taught me about standing up for what I believed in. I was going against everything my parents believed in—loving a woman. So many letters my father typed to me, from the time I was sixteen to that very day, were filled with declarations about my courage to be a leader and to say what I thought, regardless of what people said. I felt I was letting him down with my deceits—that he would expect me to tell the truth regardless of the cost. But this price was much higher than I could bear. Homosexuality was a sin. It was against the law. It was a sign you were mentally ill. People were ostracized for being gay. People lost their parents and their friends. People were fired. I couldn't conceive of dealing with the ramifications of my truth. Death would be preferable.

Back in my room, their words churned in my head. I feared telling Nicky the details because it would show what a coward I was, so I summarized the gist of it instead. I remember that we stood with arms around each other and cried. It was hard to look her in the eye; I was fearful she would know that I had betrayed our love in an effort to protect us both. She spent the few remaining nights before her father came to get her in her own room.

I helped her dad carry her things outside to his car, and Nicky came down with us on our last trip with the boxes. "Thanks for taking such good care of my little girl," Mr. King said as he got behind the wheel. Nicky and I leaned into each other as we hugged goodbye; the imprint of her hand on my back left an invisible tattoo.

"I love you," I whispered.

"I love you, too," she said, and then she stepped away and got in. She reached her hand out the window, and our fingertips brushed against each other as the car pulled away.

Instead of returning to the dorm, I walked down to the railroad tracks where we used to walk together, dazed and bereft about all that had happened between us, the power of our feelings, the agony of this secret, and the indignity induced by the confrontation by my peers. I told myself this was for the best and that we would both go on to marry guys like we were supposed to, looking for, in them, what we had found in each other. Head down, staring at the rails, I trudged, tears splashing on my boots, until the sun went down and I made my way back to the dorm in the dark, wondering how I could ever live an authentic life in a society that demanded me to lie in order to survive.

chapter 7

in the wilder- ness

Somehow, I made it through the remaining few weeks until school was out in mid-April, and I went home to my summer job in Detroit Diesel's secretarial pool. The RAs' confrontation continued to haunt me. Their words, a constant echo in my head, brought bouts of anxiety. When their voices subsided, Reverend Mitchell would take over with his threats of hell and damnation. Walking into the women's lounge on a break one day, I heard colleagues laughing at a joke: "What do you call a lesbian who lives up north?" Everyone looked up, smiling, but no one guessed at the answer. "A Klondyke," said the joke teller, laughing out loud. I sat down and opened my book, not knowing if they were trying to send me a secret message or if they were just revealing their own prejudices. I smiled along, sure to let them know I was one of them.

Every time I was called into someone's office to take dictation, I feared they would fire me because someone had told them that I was gay. If I was at home and the phone rang, I was certain that someone was calling my parents to tell them that I was a lesbian. When total strangers whispered near me on the street, I was sure they were talking about me. Peace eluded me everywhere.

Mike came the first two weekends I was home, and his presence comforted me even though he had no direct knowledge of what I had been through at school. He was solid, always there, eager to help, willing to do anything that made me happy.

Nicky and I talked on the phone, and I made the trip by train to see her at the beginning of May. Our powerful attraction remained in spite of the distance and continued to cause conflicted feelings in me that I did my best to compartmentalize. On this visit we spent the night together in her single bed and cherished the moments we had alone, holding each other in silence, fearful her parents might hear us in their bedroom next door. I worked hard to drive thoughts of Mike out of my head along with the threats of Reverend Mitchell in this small sacred space where our bodies could lie tangled together beneath the sheets and the sweet smell of her skin melted away my fear and anxiety, even if just for a few hours. Each time we parted was like ripping a Band-Aid off a wound, taking part of the scab with it.

By the middle of May, I had come down with mono, too, and had to quit my job. Fear that someone would figure out that I had gotten it from Nicky overwhelmed me. My illness kept me from seeing either Mike or Nicky for a few weeks as the doctor prescribed total rest. Rather than stay in bed, I spent six weeks lying on the beach at Kensington Metro Park, sleeping most of the day. My small consolation was a fabulous tan in time to be a radiant attendant at my brother's wedding in late June.

I still wasn't fully recovered when I joined my parents on the drive to Stevensville, where the wedding took place. They dropped me off at Mike's in Kalamazoo, and the two of us continued the trip in his car. I was happy to see him, hopeful each time we met that the magic I felt with Nicky would one day appear between us. So far it hadn't.

The small Lutheran church was simple, with a bare wooden stage at the front of the sanctuary that served as the altar. Folding chairs were aligned in neat rows set back from the platform, and makeshift steps were covered in tan cloth so the wedding party could step easily up to the stage where Jim and his fiancée, Laurie, would marry.

My brother rarely dressed up, and he looked both handsome and young in his dark navy three-piece suit with a white boutonniere, his thin neck jutting out from a marginally ironed shirt. He stood self-consciously with his cuffed pants barely reaching his shoes, his wrists exposed at the ends of too-short sleeves, his hands cupped by his sides.

On his way to becoming a chemistry professor, Jim could recite formulas in his sleep, knowing most about the chemical reactions resulting from mixing two compounds in a lab and little or nothing about the chemistry of relationships. My mother was certain he would be the last to marry, not just of her two children, but of everyone she knew. He had never dated in high school, and he didn't date in college until his junior year, when he took a ship abroad to study in Germany and met his wife-to-be, also an exchange student. When he brought Laurie home for Christmas, I liked her instantly and felt in many ways I had come to know her better in a few visits than I had known my brother after living with him for years.

As one of the bridesmaids, I waited at the front with the others as the organist played "Here Comes the Bride" and felt my eyes moisten as Laurie, beaming, glided down the aisle on her father's arm, her lace mantilla floating behind her. The music alone was a powerful elixir, inducing an overwhelming desire to have a marriage ceremony myself. I looked over at Mike sitting in the audience and imagined standing at the altar with him one day, the envy of the crowd, his tanned face highlighting his attractive features. Even then I noticed my pride was related to the jealousy of others in obtaining him as a prize rather than my irresistible desire to be with him. He was everything anyone could want. Maybe I would want him too in that way if we just kept at it.

My reverie was broken as a female soloist began to sing a song about love, which was followed by a reading from the Bible. Then the minister began the official part of the ceremony as he addressed my brother and Laurie directly. There was little prelude to speaking the vows, and I listened as Laurie repeated after the celebrant: "I, Lauren, take you, James, to be my wedded husband, to have and to hold, from this day forward, for better or for worse, for richer, for poorer, in sickness and in health, to love and to cherish—until death do us part." Then Jim said his vows, there was a prayer, and it was over. It was such a big promise for such a few short sentences. I wondered whether people realized what they were saying.

We stayed for the reception of punch and cake at the church and then said goodbye to Jim and Laurie and my folks. Mike and I headed back to the parking lot and got into his car. I hadn't seen Nicky since May, when I took the train to visit. Unable to resist the temptation, since we were only forty-five minutes from South Bend where she lived, I looked at Mike, and in my most persuasive and cheerful voice I asked if we could drive down and see Nicky. It wasn't on the way home, but that didn't matter.

Certain she would be there and happy to see me, I didn't bother to call. The adrenalin had already started to pump at the prospect of even a few hours with her. Mike looked at me with a slight smile and furrowed brow as I kept talking about how much fun it would be. Even I couldn't believe I was asking him to do this, but I missed her terribly, and though we frequently talked on the phone, her absence in my life left a void that nothing filled. From his desire to make me happy, he gave in.

Mike backed out of the parking lot and turned toward signs leading to Highway 31 South. I was playful with him in the car, my enthusiasm boosted by his agreement to take a side trip. He was worried I might not be well enough, knowing that when Nicky and I got together, we had a tendency to get fired up. He asked if I was up to it and expressed his concern about a possible relapse. I assured him I would be fine, hardly able to contain my elation when he said we could go. Even with all that had happened, I couldn't stay away. And outside of school, I felt freer—no one was looking over my shoulder and monitoring my whereabouts.

Forty minutes later we pulled into her driveway. I leapt from the car to her front door and knocked as I hollered through the screen, "Anybody home?"

Mike joined me on the porch as Nicky flew down the stairs. It was evident in her greeting that she was thrilled to see me. She opened the screen door wide and let us in.

Her folks appeared and said hello to us both, and then her mother came over and gave me a big hug before inviting us for dinner. Mike was about to say no when Nicky piped up and asked if I could spend the night, cajoling him to let me stay, given that he got to have much more time with me and she hadn't seen me in weeks. Mike looked at me and asked what I wanted to do, and though it was apparent he wasn't crazy about the prospect, I admitted I wanted to stay. Overriding my feelings of duty to him, I suggested I could take the first train back to Kalamazoo in the morning.

I walked him out to the car and reassured him of how much I loved him and that I just needed some time with my friend to catch up. We kissed goodbye, and I went back into the house. Nicky loaned me some shorts and a T-shirt, and after dinner we borrowed her dad's car and headed for the Howard Johnson motel. We scoped out the scene around the outdoor swimming pool; then I stood watch as she scaled the fence, motioning me to follow. I scrambled up behind her, threw my leg over the top, and lowered myself down. We did things together I would never do alone, and the thrill of being one step outside of sanity was a rush. Once on the other side, we shed our outer clothes and left them in a pile. We had worn bathing suits underneath our shorts, so were good to go for a dip. Nicky went immediately to the deep end and dove into the pool. I didn't know how to swim very well, so I lowered myself into the shallow end. It wasn't that warm, and I could feel goose bumps rising on my arms and legs.

"Teach me how to do that," I said to Nicky as she swam toward me after her third dive. She hopped out on the side and took my hand and led me toward the deeper end, where she showed me how to position myself with one knee on the edge of the pool and the other leg bent in a half squat. "Just lean over and push off with your foot and fall into the water."

Fall into the water? I thought, Is she crazy? But my pride impelled me forward, and I followed her instructions. Taking in a mouthful, I struggled to raise my head out of the water, yet I was delighted that I had actually performed something like a dive.

Able to stay afloat to the other side, I jumped up out of the water and shouted out a celebratory cheer of success, forgetting that we were trespassing and wanting to remain undiscovered. We raced across the pool, laughing as we splashed water on each other and felt the magic of the moonlight shine on the glassy surface. After a half hour, we got out. Nicky pulled out a towel and slipped it over my shoulders from behind. I backed up just enough to feel her arms slide down over mine. With a firm but gentle tug she wrapped the towel tighter around me so I wouldn't get a chill. But the shivers I felt couldn't be quelled with a terry cloth cover. They ran through my body like the current of a river carrying me away to a familiar place.

She put a towel around herself, sat down in a lounge chair, and beckoned me to sit in front of her. She pulled me back until I was leaning up against her—our heads tilted upward toward the sky. Her arms reached across my chest, and she drew me closer as I laid my head back. The night air was cool; the lights of the hotel loomed over the hedges. Mike's face flashed across my mind, and I allowed the image to drift away. While looking at the stars, the song "How Great Thou Art" came to mind:

Oh Lord my God,
When I in awesome wonder,
Consider all the worlds
Thy hands have made;
I see the stars,
I hear the rolling thunder,
Thy power throughout
This universe displayed . . .

It was the theme song for Billy Graham's Crusades, sung by George Beverly Shea. I used to listen to it with my dad when it was broadcast on the radio. The shimmering dots of light in the heavens took me back to that verse, and I longed for the comfort it had once brought—the belief that there was a God watching out for us and that his formidable powers would protect rather than annihilate. Now the words seemed more threatening. I closed my eyes and let go of all that came before and all that would come after this single second—aware only of my weight falling into Nicky and the love I felt between us.

I took the early train to Kalamazoo as promised; Mike met me at the station, and we drove to Milham Park. Our preferred meal was a Whopper from Burger King, and we picked up a couple on our way. As we walked toward our favorite bridge, we saw a cluster of baby ducks scramble to get in line behind their mother as she led them to the water's edge. Each one looked like a handful of feathers on legs as they waddled along. We both burst out laughing at the sight. My time with Nicky made me feel more relaxed, knowing she was okay and that the magic between us was still there. Oddly, Mike got more of me because of my time spent with her. It didn't make sense, but it was true.

I returned to my parents' house by train later that evening and on Monday took up my daily ritual of lying on the sand and wondering about the nature of God and why he would make people attracted to each other if they could never be together. Was life just one big test after another? Was he laughing up there at the world's suffering? Were we all such pitiful sinners that we didn't deserve happiness, ever? No answers came to console me, and I felt weary not knowing what to believe.

On Sundays I attended church with my parents, as I always had. Returning to that physical structure reminded me how my faith had changed over the past fifteen years. As a small child I did have faith greater than a mustard seed and believed the many Bible stories I was told. The minister often talked of God's presence in the sanctuary, and I would crane my neck, stare at the ceiling, and look for him hiding in the tiny crevices next to the giant beams that held the roof up, or I would imagine I could feel him floating above the congregation like a stream of invisible smoke.

To have faith meant to believe in things that you couldn't see—a message I heard at church and at home. My parents' trust in that invisible force was evident, but my knowledge of how to apply it was lacking; at the age of seven or eight, I had stood confidently on the front porch with my arms outstretched, telling my parents I would stay outside during the tornado warning because I had faith God would protect me should one actually come.

Though the messages of fire and brimstone frightened me, church music brought me great comfort. The hymns "Amazing Grace," "The Old Rugged Cross," "I Come to the Garden Alone," when sung by the congregation, lifted my heart and filled me with peace. When I shut my eyes, I imagined angels spreading a bed of comforters for me. Through music I found a God I could love. I memorized all the names of the books of the Bible and could recite them upon request along with legions of verses from the Old and New Testament.

At night my dad would come and tuck me into bed and say prayers with me. Sitting in the darkness, he would share about how he had strayed from God and how losing his vision was God's way of bringing him back to the Lord. It made me scared that something like that could happen to me if I drifted; and while he meant it as a life lesson about himself, it created trepidation in me.

As the minister rambled on, I recalled the night my father got sick. Sometimes I had nightmares reliving the scene as a four-year-old awakened by the creaking of my parents' bedroom door and the sound of footsteps shushing across the bare floor. My mother was on the phone and spoke in crisp sentences. "We need an ambulance at 12222 Mansfield, between Capital Street and Oshea Park—it is a dead end. Please hurry; my husband is having a convulsion."

I peeked out of the door and heard my father moan. He was not in the bedroom, but lying on the couch, covered with a red plaid bedspread. Though the light was dim, I could see his body jerk under the covers. My mother scurried around as she tossed my father's clothes in the suitcase on the bed. She explained that my daddy was sick and they were coming to take him to the hospital. Listening but not understanding, I picked up the whisker brush in his toiletries bag and pushed it around on my face like my daddy did when he shaved. I smelled the sweet scent of the lather, a momentary comfort.

The shrill sound of a siren outside was interrupted by a bold knock at the door. Two men in white coats sprung through. They rolled the stretcher next to the couch and covered my father's face with a yellow terrycloth towel. My heart pounded faster. A rush of fear raced through the room like voltage freed from a toaster cord. Flickering red lights bounced off our walls. The painting of the farmhouse in the snow over the couch was tilted to one side, and the garish red lights made it look like a haunted house.

My body quivered—not because of the cold, but because of the dreamlike quality of the panic set off inside that made me feel like I was a roaring river tumbling toward a waterfall. The men in uniform wrapped the towel tighter around my father's head as they lifted him off of the couch onto the skinny stretcher and then wheeled him out of the house and down the stairs.

Our live-in housekeeper, Mrs. Powell, and I were left standing in the living room. "Everything is going to be all right," she said as she put her arm around me and steered me back to my bed. I heard the words, but I didn't believe them even then. "Oh, don't worry, sweetie, they are going to fix him. Now go back to sleep." But I couldn't sleep; my heart was pounding and my tummy was turning over like it was filled with rotten food.

My father was in a coma for weeks, and when he finally woke up, he could no longer see normally. He'd suffered brain damage from an allergic reaction to sulfa, the medication the doctor had given him earlier in the day. If God could do something like that to my father, the best person I knew, what would he do to me?

My father's explanation of his illness combined with direct threats from the minister were inconsistent with the more balanced views of my mother, who shared stories of loving to dance at the Greystone Ballroom or taking trips with her single girlfriends on local coed cruises around Lake Michigan. It was clear in her retelling of these tales that she enjoyed a few worldly pleasures without the threat of hell and damnation befalling her. But the constant hammering about sin won out and ignited an internal conflict that lasted through my adolescent years to the present. It was impossible to reconcile my evolving attraction to women with the Baptist church's rigid thought forms about sexuality. If I was a lesbian, this choice would set me on the fast track to Hell. To agree with the church was to defy my soul. To trust myself was to let go of the only God I knew. Either choice was a bad one.

The church, once so familiar as a child, had become foreign and disturbing. There was a new minister now that Reverend Mitchell had left, but many of the elders' familiar messages of fire and brimstone and the need to be saved remained. After years away at college, and given my increased awareness of social issues, this religion began to seem quite lacking. Deeper doubts arose about Christianity and its legitimacy. It seemed man had created God in his image rather than the other way around, or the portrayal of him wouldn't be so schizophrenic. How could any God be absolutely loving and hateful at the same time? How could such a being have his son die on the cross for your sins, but want to punish you for everything you did, rendering the offering of Christ invalid?

The church's narrow focus on its congregation's sin and redemption left it mute on the upheaval spinning about the world: the implications of the Vietnam War, our role as Christians in supporting racial justice, or the meaning of loving our neighbors despite our differences, be it a black family or a gay couple. There were no visible members of either group in our sheltered church home.

Mike came many weekends through the rest of the summer, and I was grateful for the familiarity of his steady presence. The Detroit Tigers were really hot that year, and my mom won the city lottery for a chance to purchase two tickets to the World Series, which she gave to Mike and me. Though it was the year Denny McLain won thirty-one games, we had the unfortunate experience of watching him lose one of only six that year.

Nicky and I stayed in touch through the summer, occasionally visiting by train to see one another. Those times were bittersweet—filled with the joy of intimacy and emotional attachment yet fraught with the underlying nervousness of being caught and the sadness of each departure. I strived to transfer the feelings I had for Nicky to Mike, as though they were funds in a bank that could be moved from one account to another. My sense of loyalty to him—along with my fear of God's retribution and my parents' discovery—eventually scared me straight for awhile. The hardest thing to get over was the hatred I felt for myself—not for loving Nicky, but for being too cowardly to admit it in public when confronted.

In September, Nicky transferred to Indiana University in South Bend so she could live with her parents and save money. As a result, we spoke less often and eventually grew apart—not because the love had faded, but because I couldn't tolerate the pain. Being involved in activities that demanded little emotional effort were a relief, and I sought out experiences that required nothing of me—lost in the numbness I felt without Nicky in my life.

Without the capacity to reconcile such profound feelings for a woman with the rigidity of Baptist theology, I was a captive prisoner to my own thoughts—a struggle I didn't have the skill or knowledge to win. The Church was Goliath, and I had no David within me.

The freedom I longed for in loving Nicky would remain out of reach.

chapter 8

will you marry me?

t was difficult to return to school alone. There was no telling who had started the rumors, making me skittish around everyone in the dorm. Then, there were the memories of Nicky, lingering like ghosts in the hallways, the cafeteria, and the rec room, at once a constant presence and an unabated emptiness.

In most heterosexual love relationships there is a marked beginning and end, allowing you to first express the joy of falling in love and revel in your friends' happiness that you have found someone. And, if you should break up with the guy of your dreams, these same friends come to grieve with you in the loss of this special connection. They know your heart is broken, and they are present to help you heal. Because my relationship with Nicky was secret, there was no acknowledged beginning, no shared recognition of the love we shared together, and then no understanding of or support in the immense loss of her leaving. Because the true nature of our relationship was invisible to others from the beginning, I was alone in my sorrow when it was gone.

In an effort to ease the emptiness, I refocused my attention on a double major in sociology and business education with the intention of becoming a high school teacher. Though my original motivation in transferring to a four-year program was for social reasons, it seemed, with the proper focus, I could finish with a teaching degree. This would require an extra year, but I welcomed the space to revitalize my relationship with Mike as I worked toward graduating with a profession other than that of a secretary. I was assigned a new roommate, a transfer student from New York who knew nothing of my past. We got along well, though I spent much of my time at the library just to be away from the haunting memories.

Whenever Mike came over, I made sure we studied in the dining hall, so people could see us together. We double dated with my sorority sisters and went to parties where we were visible to others. We attended church and spent time with his older friends—all of this public display intended to broadcast that I was a happily partnered, heterosexual girl. But I felt afraid and abandoned—first by myself and then by the people I thought were my friends, but most significantly by the God I was taught to believe in. There was no comfort for me in that faith because there was no room for the person I feared myself to be. All the traits my father admired—love and kindness, compassion and determination—were still solidly a part of me, yet they seemed inconsequential in comparison to the sin of loving a woman.

In spite of my guardedness, I made a new friend during the winter of 1969. Julie was also a sociology major, which made it natural for us to regularly hang out. She was smart and insightful, with short, brown, unruly hair that curled in multiple directions. She wore it closely cropped to her head just to keep it manageable. Her face was angular and youthful, with dimples that made her look even younger when she smiled. Her blue eyes were set beneath thin eyebrows, creating a soft yet strong presence. Introverted and observant, she surprised me with keen perceptions, often about what seemed a casual comment I made in conversation. I had found a way to have a new pal and stay focused on my commitment to Mike. Yet the fear I lived with moment to moment served as a constant reminder of the unintended consequences of letting my emotions overrun my rational thinking. I worked hard to construct a persona that projected confidence and comfort on the outside, while on the inside I was an unruly mess.

When the school year was over, I returned to my job at Detroit Diesel, and Julie took a job at a tennis camp a half hour from Kalamazoo. Our friendship deepened through letters; with both of us loving to write, we were able to carry on the same level of conversation in print as we had in person. She was thoughtful, poetic, and creative—always including magazine pictures or cartoons in her letters that illustrated her thoughts. She visited me once in Detroit for a weekend, and Mike and I went to see her at the tennis camp. We each desired depth in friendship and treasured our time together. Her capacity for closeness helped to ease the sadness I felt in Nicky's absence.

When I returned to school in September 1969, I got an apartment off campus with a couple of friends. I had saved enough money to purchase a used 1966 VW Bug for eleven hundred dollars, for transportation back and forth to class and to do my student teaching in a town thirty miles away. This was a new feeling of freedom on all fronts. I was actually on track to graduate in the spring of 1970. I breathed more easily outside the dorm, no longer wondering who thought I was gay. Of greatest relief was that Mike and I were moving closer to being engaged.

Advice on marriage remained at the top of my mother's letters, most of which involved suggestions on how to be decorous around men—with Mike, in particular, so he could feel good about himself. My mom was her own woman long before there was a feminist movement—a person who expected to be treated with respect by men and wasn't shy about addressing their weak points. She often told a story about a guy she dated who complained to her that she gave him an inferiority complex. To this she boldly replied, "You had one long before I met you."

But when it came to giving me advice about the male gender, and about marriage in particular, I would receive letters like the following:

> *It makes parents concerned about the type of husband you'll have, hopefully he will be as full of zest for living as yourself and he will understand you completely . . .*
>
> *When I realize how God blessed me with a wonderful husband, in spite of myself, I feel sure you will fare well too. It means a lot when the man loves you completely, because their work comes first, but you're important too. If you can appreciate a man and show it, doesn't it do wonders for your relationship? Have you heard the record,* Be Good to Your Man?

I'm sure she meant the song "Stand by Your Man," but either way, it wasn't the melody she sang in her approach to dating, and I couldn't understand why she thought it should be mine.

I wondered, Who is this woman? The mother I lived with and after whom I modeled myself was fiercely independent, sassy, and sure of herself, someone who wouldn't dream of being "less than" in any category, just to please a man. And the father I lived with loved her exactly that way and wouldn't have married her if she was hanging all over him always trying to make him feel good about himself.

The mother who showed up in letters like this was perplexing and annoying. She was in tune with the times of the sixties, in our working-class orbit where the majority of young girls in our church were marching toward wedded bliss without an after-thought. Even though the feminist movement had been launched with the publication of *The Feminine Mystique* by Betty Frie-dan in 1963 and the founding of the National Organization for Women in 1966, no one in my social network was awakened by these early calls for the equal partnership of women in Ameri-can society.

For centuries women had been economically tied to men and rarely had the means to do anything but marry if they didn't want to live in poverty. Even if women could find a way to sup-port themselves, they risked social inferiority because of their singlehood past a certain age. It didn't matter how smart they were; it mattered how beautiful they were—how adept at dimin-ishing themselves to whatever degree necessary to succeed as wives, their most significant role.

I, too, was indoctrinated this way, despite living in a family that had shifted the paradigm in response to my father's illness. Popular television shows like *Father Knows Best, The Adventures of Ozzie and Harriet,* and *Leave It to Beaver* drove home the one acceptable role for women. The wives in all these shows were incessantly cheerful, immaculately groomed, wore pearls and heels while doing household chores, and lived in spotless houses where young children (mostly boys) never messed things up and where a four-course meal was served at five every evening. The fathers were the source of all wisdom, dispensing moral lessons for their children at the dinner table, and the mothers were end-less wellsprings of love and support for everyone in the family. At the end of the day, the parents would have meaningful con-versations as they sat up in their twin beds across from each other with pajamas buttoned up to their necks. It was a kind of hypnotic trance that lulled girls into a false sense of real-ity. And, even though my family wasn't like that, I somehow imagined during the fifties and sixties that every other family on my street was, that ours was only different because my father was ill and my mother had to work. I didn't realize that almost no one had a family like that.

My mother reinforced that television model, constantly encouraging me to meet the right guy. The second year of our relationship Mike accepted Christ as his savior. Now that he was "saved," he was the benefactor of my mother's counsel because he had become the perfect catch. Not a week went by during my college years that she didn't tell me about some girl my age in our church who was either having a shower, getting married, or having a baby. And the emphasis was always on the wedding itself—bridesmaids, color choices, the site of the reception. Little consideration was given to the marriage, to shared values, or a desire to have children or understanding how to care for them.

My mother's letters, the social mores of the time, and my deep yearning to not be a lesbian all pushed me toward a wedded path upon graduation. The day I finally made up my mind, Mike and I were sitting in his blue Volkswagen Bug out in front of my apartment. It was a bright, chilly November afternoon in 1969. We were discussing the future of our relationship, now that I would graduate in April. While I can recall the image of us scrunched together in the small space, it seems odd that I don't remember any of the specific details of such an important discussion, except for one: By the time I got out of the car, I had agreed to marry him. I don't remember how he asked me, nor do I remember feelings of joy and excitement. It seemed he was part of my destiny and that graduation from college meant it was time to grow up. I was in a constant internal battle with myself over the compelling draw I felt for women friends, though I had not acted on any other feelings after the catastrophic experience of being with Nicky, even though I felt an occasional wave of desire—especially with

Julie. It seemed the only way out of that recurring temptation was to make a commitment to a guy and to stick with it.

I designed my own ring and spent hours drawing different pictures of the ideal symbol reflecting our love. I settled on a tear-shaped design in gold that looked like a peace symbol going one way with the diamond nestled in the lower portion of the ring. Then if you turned it upside down, it looked like a rose with the diamond becoming the bloom of the flower. Certainly one of a kind, it achieved the desired oohs and aahs from friends. My time might have been better spent trying to understand what we had in common and why we wanted to marry. I had no idea how to create an adult relationship. In that era, people frequently talked about girls going to college to get their "MRS degree," an accomplishment that was viewed with greater admiration than the BA or BS. My mother had taught me the characteristics to look for in a husband. Was he handsome? Check. Was he respectful? Check. Was he kind? Check. Was he a Christian? Check. Mike was all those things and more. I was good to go. All I wanted—dared to want—was to feel normal.

We would marry in June, two months after my graduation, and I would look for a teaching job in Kalamazoo. My pending degree was a monumental accomplishment—an achievement that far exceeded the associate's degree I originally hoped to obtain. This was more than a backup plan for me; I wanted to be a teacher, and I had worked hard for that opportunity. And, through feedback from my student teaching mentors, I had developed the confidence that I would be great at it.

In April a few of my pals threw me a bridal shower and, in addition to my friends, invited my mother, Mike's mom, and two of his sisters. I awoke that morning feeling nauseous and unable to take a deep breath. With effort, I made my way out of bed and started to run a bath in the giant claw-foot tub. As I stood and watched the bubbles expand across the top of the water, I thought about my life at school coming to a close. The thought of graduating was scary—the thought of getting married scarier still. Then there were the fears about who I might actually be that I tried to conceal, even from myself.

My mind turned to memories of Nicky. There had been no final goodbye, just a drifting away, like taffy pulling in opposite directions, stretching until it separated completely. I thought about all the time we spent together—the walks, the late nights in my room talking, watching the matches burn, our bus ride to Benton Harbor, swimming in the dark at the Howard Johnson pool, and the day she left school. Was it even possible that someone would ever know me like she did? I wondered if she was engaged by now, too.

Julie and I had also grown much closer in the last year, and I felt enlivened by the time we spent together. Her intellect and curiosity were enticing—something I missed in my relationship with Mike. The richness of my conversations with girlfriends was always more stimulating and emotionally exciting than discussions I had had with any man. The women more often made me think about my purpose in life and question what I really wanted. They made me dig deeper for the truth.

It wasn't that I wasn't attracted to men. I knew I had been in love with Charlie, and my love for Mike was genuine. But with women, I felt most understood, and my craving for emotional intimacy was most satisfied. The men of my era were trapped in their own social paradigms, where John Wayne served as the model and any gesture toward vulnerability was perceived as weakness. There was not yet a corresponding men's movement that encouraged their emotional development or any desire on their part to acknowledge women's equality.

Soaking in the tub, I sought comfort in the softness of the

bubbles until Kathy, my off-campus roommate knocked on the bathroom door and reminded me of the time. Without enthusiasm I roamed through my closet and selected my beige jumper and dark brown blouse to wear. People would arrive in forty minutes, so I quickly dressed and went out to meet my hosting friends. I took a tour around the apartment, moving first to the food table, with tea sandwiches and a variety of salads surrounding a large cake with "Congratulations Carol and Mike" scrawled in cursive on the frosting. Another table, set aside for all the gifts, was draped with a white curtain from the bedroom. I felt anxious and disconnected as I wandered through the space and wondered why I didn't feel happier.

I greeted my mother at the door.

"Hi, honey. How are you?" She leaned in and gave me a hug, then in the next breath said, "Oh, Carol. You aren't going to wear that, are you? Why don't you wear the green dress you wore to the mother-and-daughter banquet last year?"

Not in the mood for an argument, I smiled and thanked her for her suggestion and just moved on. "Do I look all right?" I kept asking everyone who passed by until Julie took me by the hand and led me to a chair, sat me down, and took a seat next to me.

"Are you okay?" she asked.

"My stomach is a mess."

"I think that's natural," she said, putting her hand on my knee in a reassuring gesture. "Try to focus on something that makes you happy."

My only thought was that I should feel joyful on this occasion, but I didn't.

Once everyone arrived, Kathy and Julie led the group in some silly shower games before I opened the presents. Through the whole afternoon, I forced smiles of appreciation and gratitude while my gut flared in opposition to the whole affair. Before leaving, I walked my mother to the car. "It was such a lovely party," she said as I hugged her goodbye. "You two make such a handsome couple."

I wanted to grab her by the hand and say, "You don't understand. I'm dying inside. I don't know what I'm doing. I'm scared to death and not sure I love him as much as I loved Nicky." Instead, I said, "Thanks, Mom. It was great to see you."

My roommates moved out of my apartment after graduation. I continued to live there while working part-time as a teacher at a private business school in the evening and as a substitute in public school during the day. This would be a temporary living arrangement until after the wedding in June. As the weeks went on, I felt more confined, trapped. One night in May, Julie presented me with a gift: a Raggedy Ann doll inside a meticulously wrapped cardboard box. I had one when I was younger and always loved her. Instead of the traditional dress of blue gingham with a white apron, this Raggedy Ann was in hand-sewn denim overalls with a white turtleneck, her pudgy hands sticking out at the ends of the sleeves. The outfit was custom made by Julie herself.

"You looked so nervous at your shower, I thought you needed something to hold on to."

"She's beautiful," I said, staring at her and noticing the fine stitching on the overalls and the detail on her white turtleneck. She made her with such love and attention, not only to the creation of Raggedy's outfit, but to my emotional needs, as well. Her insights were uncanny in this way—always seeing what was invisible to others. I leaned over and kissed her on the cheek. "You're really something. I will treasure her always." She was right: I did need something to hang on to. I was no more comfortable now about the thought of getting married than I had been at the shower. I held the doll with one hand and patted her bright red hair with the other as I tried to untangle the emotional wiring that unraveled inside me.

Later that week, I went for a long walk in Milham Park and climbed the giant pine tree at the edge of the bridge that Mike and I had climbed on our first date. I watched the ducks fight over the scraps of food others tossed their way, just like they had the first time we came here. I sat for more than an hour scratching my way through the memories of my five-year stint in college, hoping to be touched by a magic elixir that would bring clarity and peace.

I had never been with anyone as devoted as Mike, or anyone who showed up in such a committed way. It was Mike working side by side with me at three o'clock in the morning twisting the last of the fake carnations onto the wire mesh around the giant goose that laid the golden egg in preparation for the homecoming parade the next morning because I was in charge of that project for my sorority. And it was Mike who jumped in the car with me and drove a hundred and fifty miles to Detroit for a surprise visit to my mother who was feeling down one evening only to jump in the car again at five o'clock in the morning to get back in time for class. It was Mike who stood in the freezing cold while I chiseled the shape of a chipmunk out of ice for the snow sculpture at my dorm one year, patiently handing me the tool I needed and pouring more water on the finished product to keep it frozen. And it was Mike who endured my spontaneous trips to Benton Harbor and South Bend so I could spend time with Nicky. There wasn't anyone better than him—as a man or as a human being. It wasn't that he was not enough; it was that he wasn't what I needed.

No such elixir came through my reflections, and no mystical insights dropped from the sky. What did come was the sorrowful realization I dreaded to affirm: I had to break the engagement.

That afternoon, Mike and I went out for lunch and then returned to my apartment, where we sat out front in his car. Though Mike met all the criteria I had been taught to seek in a husband and was the kindest man I knew, I had never felt about him the way I felt about Nicky; I didn't even have the same ani- mated feelings for him that I had for Julie.

The sting of this self-acknowledgment was equaled only by the ache that arose at the thought of telling him. I knew he was crazy about me—for reasons that were often difficult to grasp, given my behavior—and I feared the news would devastate him. The knowledge that he could recover from short-term pain more readily than the harm caused by a marriage built on secrets was the only thought that gave me the courage to follow through.

Since it was impossible for me to tell him about my attrac- tion to women, I told him a partial truth. Fidgeting with my keys, I could feel the words catch in my throat. "You know I love you, Mike, and these past three years have been wonderful. You have always treated me with respect and kindness."

There was a long pause, and my voice softened to a whisper. The look on his face told me that he knew the next line would be painful to hear. Avoiding his eyes, I looked down at my keys and went on. "I don't know how to say this, but I am just not ready to get married right now."

The silence weighed on us. The gray of the day pressed through the windowpane as I blinked to keep back the tears. My heart was still pumping, but I felt cold and empty, knowing I was not only killing his dream, but crushing the biggest part of my life that made me feel normal. My face was hot; my hands were freezing. The scene was unfolding in slow motion—no sound, no rustling in our seats, no words coming from him for what seemed like an hour, though I am sure it was only minutes. There was just the internal booming sound of my head throbbing.

"You know I love you," he said. "What if we waited a little longer? We don't have to get married right now."

I wanted to cave in and say, "Okay—let's wait and see." But I knew I had waited too long already, and no matter how much more time we wallowed in this never-never land of my noncommitment, things wouldn't change. To go on would be like wounding an animal, then dragging it behind you for miles before you let it die. "I love you too—and always will. I just can't commit to anything right now and don't know if or when that will change. You deserve more than that."

Stillness hovered in the small space between us as we both stared through the windshield wishing things were different. I didn't know how to love him in the way I loved women. I didn't know how to manufacture those same thrilling states of longing and hunger for him that had coursed through my body at the sight of Nicky, or the feelings that I resisted having for Julie when in her presence. Wishing it so for three years had failed, and I couldn't go on pretending. I slipped the ring off of my finger and held it out for him to take back.

"It was made for you. I hope you'll keep it and wear it sometime on your other hand."

"Are you sure?" I asked, bewildered, but grateful. Even if he changed his mind later, I would keep it for now.

Looking into his face, I saw the hurt my message had caused, the blue of his eyes blurred by tears. I held his hand and felt the familiar roughness I had felt the first night we went out. They were thick and sturdy, comforting and capable hands. There was nothing more to say. I wanted to wish the ache away;

I wanted the incessant pounding to stop and for the sting to be eased by something—anything. But nothing could touch this pain for either of us. So we continued to sit there, both accepting the end but neither making a move to get out of the car.

"I will take care of sending all the gifts from the shower back," I said.

"I can help if you like."

Doing anything more together felt dangerous. It had taken all I had to make the break, and, despite my resolve, I was unsure of my ability to follow through. "Thanks, but this is my doing, and I need to clean up the mess I've made."

Finally, I moved toward him and kissed him goodbye, then reached for the door handle to exit the car. As always, he got out, walked around, and opened the door for me. I made my way alone up the stairs to my apartment. Closing the front door behind me, I wondered if I had just made the biggest mistake of my life, but the calm that came over me as I sat on the couch affirmed that I had not.

chapter 9

road
trip

Julie and I took a road trip to Florida in June to take my
mind off the wedding I wasn't going to have. We drove
her new lemon yellow Datsun, a gift from her father for
graduation. I hadn't lost my penchant for sunbathing since the
days Gina and I spread out on picnic tables slathered in baby oil.
Advancing to an oceanside version of tanning made the prospect
thrilling. I was ecstatic to get out of town, to listen to the hum
of tires on the freeway, to be soothed by salty air and ocean
breezes. A major destination on our way south was Knoxville,
Tennessee, to visit my Great-Aunt Noreen. I couldn't wait for
them to meet, and I entertained Julie on the way with memories
of my favorite relative.

Aunt Noreen was my grandmother's sister. I first met her
when I was twelve when she attended my grandma's funeral.
She was dressed then in a purple tweed suit with a fake mink
collar and a wide-brimmed scarlet hat with a single ostrich
feather. Her sturdy calves, partially visible below her skirt,
were anchored in the same black stacked heels my grandmother
wore—her lips painted a shade that matched her hat. A pair of

crimson gloves completed the outfit. Wisps of fine red hair swept out from underneath her headgear; her face had rivers of lines flowing in all directions. She wore round, rimless glasses, and when she smiled, a smudge of lipstick was often visible on her front tooth. Unaware that my grandma had any siblings, I was enchanted by this discovery and mesmerized by Aunt Noreen's physical presentation as well as her directness. We got on well, and my mother promised we would visit her in a few years, when my brother turned seventeen and could help with the driving.

Aunt Noreen was the only relative on my mother's side that I had the slightest interest in knowing. All of the others were distant and stuffy, but Aunt Noreen was bold and funny. Her bawdy humor and disrespect for rules was appealing to a fifteen-year-old with little concern for other's expectations. She was a shining star in the dark night of extended family members whose greatest joy in life, it seemed, was finding fault with me. But she knew how to talk to me, and she listened to what I had to say.

My favored memory of that visit was the evening we stood out on her postage-sized patio in the chilled night air and listened to stories about my grandmother that made us wince. As she held court, she reached for a beer out of the carton on the table and popped the top. Feeling emboldened by her audacious attitude, I piped up and said, "I want a beer, too." Without flinching, she grabbed another and handed it to me, making me embarrassed not to drink at least part of it, though I knew from the sips I'd taken with Gina that I wouldn't like it. But I liked having the gumption to ask for one. My mother looked on but never said a word.

Though I refrained from telling my mother, I secretly wished Aunt Noreen had been my grandma instead of the one I got.

The roads through the mountains were much improved since

my last visit, years before, allowing us to cut off a couple hours of travel time. My excitement built as we arrived in the city and followed the directions to her address. Her mobile home was still marked by a string of Chinese lanterns made of crepe paper that hung across her patio. Her pristine white '57 Chevy was parked at its standard forty-five-degree angle on the hill in the woods, facing toward the road as though to make a quick getaway—just as I remembered it.

Aunt Noreen had been through a recent surgery, and from the moment we arrived, I sensed a difference in her. The familiar smells of ancient things mixed with perfume flooded us as we entered the living room. The same bright-colored afghans were strewn about. But her voice was different—angry and abrupt. "What took you so long? Come in and get yourselves something to eat. I already ate."

My stomach roiled, and the moisture on my palms brought chills in the evening air. This was not her customary animated voice, full of warmth and mischief. I didn't know if we should get our luggage or maybe look for a hotel. I made introductions. Then we sat down at the table, ate dinner, and joined her in the living room. She sat in her rocker, nodding off in the middle of conversation, occasionally jerking herself to attention to speak. We talked about our trip, how the roads had changed, and how happy we were to be on vacation. I sat on the couch and inhaled the smells of perfume and musty blankets. She no longer asked interesting questions; she felt distant to me, old in a somber way, more like my grandmother, with whom I was never close.

"I arranged for you to see Dr. Ruth and your Aunt Pearl," (my grandmother's other sisters), "while you are here. I don't know if I will feel well enough to come along."

I nodded graciously and said that would be nice. At 9:00 p.m. she said good night. Julie and I stayed up late, enjoying our freedom and anticipating our time at the ocean. Our laughter must have awakened her, and she shuffled out in her baggy blue flannel bathrobe, shouting. "What in the hell are you doing up at this hour? I am exhausted and trying to sleep," she said in a belittling and irritated tone. I refused to cry or offer apology, though I wanted to bolt out the door, down the steps, and back into the yellow Datsun and drive to Florida without stopping. Where was my exciting, eccentric, understanding Aunt Noreen? She left the room, and we turned out the lights. Tears stung my eyes as I pressed my face into the antique pillowcase lying on the cot across from Julie.

The next day we went out to dinner with Dr. Ruth and Pearl, plus Billie and Buddy, my cousins. We talked about the nothings that relatives talk about when they don't know each other well.

"My how you've grown," Ruth said. "How is your mother?"

Then my Aunt Pearl chimed in, "It has been so hard for her all these years with your dad being so sick and all. Could you please pass the coleslaw—I just love how they make it here."

A chorus of voices slid over each other as I sat and acted polite on the outside, though my insides felt ragged from the night before. At the end of the meal, we went back to Aunt Noreen's house—full of food, but not so full of the love I had remembered. Julie and I left the next day. After our visit, she wrote my mother a letter that caused them to break ties altogether. It would be another eight years before I learned the content of that message.

As we rolled down the road toward I-85, Julie turned off the radio and asked how I felt.

"Well, that didn't turn out like I thought it would," I said. "She used to be different—fun and funny, with a great sense of humor. I'm sorry she was so mean."

"That's okay. You should meet some of my relatives," Julie said with a laugh.

I glanced her way again and saw that she still had her eyes fixed on me.

"What are you thinking?" I asked, worried that this bad start to the vacation had really put a damper on the whole thing.

"I want to tell you something."

I had no idea what she was about to say, but I feared that she didn't want to be my friend anymore. Maybe she had heard stories about me being gay. I gripped the wheel a little tighter and waited for the bad news.

"What is it?" Jesus, I thought—just spit it out. I can take it.

"I was thinking that I would really like to kiss you."

I turned sharply in her direction to see if she was joking or if some weird spell had come over her. Not only was that the last thing I expected; it was also way beyond the last thing I wanted, and my immediate response was a resounding, "Oh, no you wouldn't." It wasn't the most sensitive approach, but I was having none of that again. I thought Julie was straight. I certainly knew that I wanted to be. What now? I wondered. Do I explain what happened to me with Nicky, and how horrible it was in spite of how wonderful it was, too? Do I admit that, even though I have been fighting against it, I am attracted to her, also? Or do I just keep my mouth shut?

I pulled off at the first rest area and stopped the car. My uneasiness increased as I turned toward her. Before I spoke, I made her promise that she would never tell anyone what I was about say. She swore that she wouldn't, and I spilled out my whole story. I told her about Nicky and the terror I felt in having those feelings because of my Christian upbringing, and about the guilt that followed me everywhere because I loved Mike and he was such a good person. I told her about the horror of being confronted by the other RAs, the dread my parents would find out, and how I was terrorized each time the phone rang at home, certain someone was calling to tell them I was gay. And that, even though I could feel the intermittent waves of attraction to her, I was not, for any reason, under any circumstance, *ever* going to act on them.

Now I felt totally exposed—first for sharing what I had done before, and second for telling her I had similar feelings toward her. She was quiet for a while as I sat nervously wishing I could roll the words I had spoken back up into my mouth.

"I'm really sorry that you were so hurt by what happened," she said. She reached over and touched my hand reassuringly. "I can understand why you would come to that decision—I just wanted you to know what I was feeling."

The problem was that I was feeling that same pull toward her and had been for months. I was sure that on a subconscious level my awareness of these feelings was part of the reason I broke my engagement with Mike. My attraction to Nicky was scary enough, but now, here it was again. With women it was so much harder because it snuck up on me. It always began as friendship, and love grew out of an intense emotional bond that was unparalleled with men. Yet I could never imagine living as a lesbian. Though I had never met one, my imaginings about gay women were the worst: I had heard stories about butch and fem partnerships, one person trying to act like a man, the other like a woman. In my mind they all rode motorcycles, smoked cigarettes, and were unemployed. God knows why I had such ridiculous ideas. They appeared to be thought forms that hung in the social ether. Wherever they came from, I couldn't see myself in that group.

The envisioned pain of acting on the lure of Julie's charm was enough to keep my promise to myself not to get involved with her throughout the vacation. No wonder she hadn't been that keen on dating Mike's brother when I introduced them last fall, though we double dated for a few months. If I were to be honest, there were signs that we were more attracted to each other than I was to most friends, even then. I remembered when we were together how close she stood to me, and the physical pleasure I derived from that. Or how she would touch me lightly in passing, seemingly by accident, and the tingling sensation that would arise as a result. The final occasion the four of us spent together was the wedding of a good friend in St. Joseph, Michigan. It was winter, and, after the reception, we'd gone to the dunes on Lake Michigan and sat in the parking lot at the beach, watching the wind and snow whip across the ice and sand. Julie was in the front seat making out with Steve, and Mike and I were in the back seat doing the same. I recalled the flash of desire I'd had to be kissing her, instead—a thought I instinctively buried the moment it came.

Now she was free to say aloud what I intuitively knew but didn't want to acknowledge. And because Julie hadn't been subject to the overpowering, harsh indoctrination of the Baptist church—or any other such religious paradigm that invoked visions of damnation for having hopes of a relationship—she had no qualms about telling me what she wanted. That made it all the harder to keep my word to myself. Our time in Florida was as healing as it was captivating with the now-open disclosure of our attraction. She was the first person I ever told about Nicky, and, as much as I had feared that level of honesty, her compassionate response was reassuring beyond any I had imagined in my terrified mind. My secret was out—even if only to one person.

We returned to Kalamazoo, and our emotional intimacy deepened as we spent more time together, as did the desire to act on the physical attraction. My yearning for depth and complexity in thought and discourse felt like an addiction—a drug that was hard to find with people in general and most especially for me with men. It was the absence of this quality in Mike that, in spite of all his other wonderful traits, made it impossible for me to marry him.

One night Julie came for dinner at my apartment and stayed to talk until it was midnight. Sitting on the couch, we shared more deeply about our childhood experiences and our plans for the future—laughing at ourselves and with each other. Each time we got up to get something, we sat back down closer together, until we were right up next to each other. My body continued to betray my will as we talked on, the rush of lust combined with tenderness reaching out to all my nerve endings—the terrible longing to touch her face, to hold her close, to yield to the hunger for physical connection. That night my intention to never sleep with a woman again was overpowered by the sweet craving of the moment. I couldn't believe I was allowing myself to drop over this cliff once more. Somehow the darkness felt like it could protect me and us from any negative outcome, and I gave in. It was the first of many nights we slept together, arms and legs entwined, loving the freedom the night allowed and wishing the sun would never rise.

Here I was, once again, splitting internally into a public and private self—two parts of me that never found a unified home. Julie's intelligence and creativity were so seductive, and physical desire seemed so natural when I was attracted to the substance of a person. Yet, even after all my doubts about Christianity, I couldn't rid myself of the shame that always descended to crush the rousing pleasure of being together. The wounds caused by loving Nicky were still too fresh and haunting, and I knew I could never be happy choosing a life that was in such opposition to my family's beliefs—and my own.

I often wished I had been raised in a household without any religion. There were legions of wonderful people walking the earth unencumbered by internal threats of punishment—people who cared for the poor, were generous to others, and worked for positive change. They were Christian in their deeds, but they didn't suffer the agony of living with a "God albatross" about their collar, robbing them of their daily joy.

I didn't know how to be brave in this situation and couldn't tell if it took greater courage to stay or to leave. What did it mean to be fearless—to follow your heart when your heart was torn in two directions? It seemed the only way to combat the power of my feelings for Julie was to find a job in another city and force myself to leave.

chapter
10

cross-roads

t took a while before a path to a new opportunity, away from Kalamazoo, opened up. In the meantime, my part-time job at the business school combined with substitute teaching was wearing on my nerves. Without Mike as a cover, I was even more petrified of being labeled a lesbian. I awoke many mornings with a churning gut and feelings of self-doubt. Though I knew it was right to break my engagement with Mike, my anxiety about marrying him was replaced with my apprehension of an uncertain future, more complicated now by my feelings toward Julie. Substituting at the local high school was not my dream job—it was an endurance contest—and I was outnumbered by, and insufficiently prepared for, thirty screaming teenagers expert in terrorizing novice teachers. I needed to get out of there for many reasons, so I intensified my job search.

As I was getting ready to leave my apartment one morning in February 1971, a small ad fell out of my pocket when I pulled out my gloves. My mother's efforts had moved temporarily from the goal of getting me married to the goal of finding me reliable work. The newspaper ad had come from her. I had already turned down a plethora of secretarial offers she had secured for me at Ford Motor Company, determined to hold out for a teaching job. I had also developed my leadership skills in college as president of my pledge class, as an RA, and as the historian in my dorm. I'd received accolades for marshaling forces to build the homecoming float for my sorority and for achieving third prize for the dorm in a campus-wide competition for best snow sculpture. A major gift of my college education had been the development of my self-confidence, which now equaled the level my father had always had in me. Though determined to discover my own way without help from outsiders, in a moment of desperation, my resolve wavered, and I picked up the ad and dialed the phone.

A gruff, gravelly voice answered on the other end. "Hello, Stokehouse here."

"Hello, my name is Carol Anderson, and I would like to apply for the teaching job at your school."

We talked for about twenty minutes before he said, "Do you know where the Burger Chef is on Dix Road?" I looked at the ad again, making sure it was for a teaching position.

"Yes," I answered cautiously.

"Well the school is right next door, but we are finishing the build-out of the space and working on the drywall. Meet me there at four o'clock next Monday."

I was elated that I had an interview for a teaching job at a private business school—a full-time position at the Danbury School of Business in Allen Park, Michigan, a Detroit suburb 130 miles away. No longer engaged to Mike, there was no need to stay in Kalamazoo, and, with Julie's and my increasing involvement, there was a very good reason to leave.

Mr. Stokehouse and I met the next week at the Burger Chef, and over french fries and a Coke, I told him of my love of teaching, my interest in helping people grow, and that I had put myself through school as a secretary so I could teach from a place of experience. He listened through to the end of my monologue, nodding his head, but not saying anything or asking any questions. In a desperate moment to punctuate my commitment, I blurted out, "I'll even help you finish the drywall if you hire me!" I think that final gesture sealed the deal.

He smiled for the first time in the interview and said, "You're hired. Can you start in two weeks?"

This was my first real position, and I was both excited and apprehensive, as I was to teach all of the classes that were offered: Shorthand, Typing, Business Math, and Personality and Poise. Typing and Shorthand were a breeze for me; Math a little questionable; but, Personality and Poise? That was going to be a stretch. My natural instincts leaned either toward matters of substance or toward athletics. I was better prepared to teach field hockey or the Inner Workings of the Soul than to educate people how to behave in superficial ways to create a positive image. But I was undaunted by the title and decided I would add my personal flair to the class and I would survive.

Like many private business schools, Danbury served a multitude of students enrolled in government programs like the Manpower Development Act, which provided training for women on welfare. The goal was to teach women skills that would equip them to secure decent jobs with decent pay, allowing them to get off of government subsidies. I had no idea what that meant, but I met the challenge with the idealism and gusto that only a twenty-three-year-old eager for permanent employment could muster.

This job also provided a way to break the intensity of my relationship with Julie. It was a driving motivation to move, now that Mike and I were not going to marry and I had no meaningful employment in Kalamazoo. I needed to leave. I hated to leave. I was more confused than ever and more tormented. I could start over in a new place with everything—a new job, a new vision for my life. And I would meet a new guy. I was sure of it.

Julie was dismayed at my departure. I was, too, but I couldn't contend with the ongoing angst that someone would find out about our relationship and I would be doomed. We agreed to remain friends and to commit to keeping that boundary while still savoring the joy we both cherished in our relationship. It was hard for both of us and especially for her, because she did not share my internal anxieties. She had no reason to stop, and I envied her for that, but, as much as I tried, I couldn't rid myself of the shame and guilt that plagued me from my fundamentalist upbringing.

I found a small apartment in Dearborn, halfway between my parents' house and my job, on an upper flat with natural light that filtered through the windows most of the day. My passion for teaching was increased by the multitude of issues these particular students—most in their thirties and forties—presented, and I was determined to see them all graduate, whatever it took.

At the end of each semester, I wrote a progress report on every student. Later David Stokehouse, the elder son of the owner, told me the leader of the Manpower program confided in him that my assessments were more astute than those of the psychologist who worked with the students. This encouragement nurtured the seeds of my emerging desire to be a psychologist and prompted me to take evening graduate classes in psychology at Marygrove College.

While the Danbury School of Business was a great place to get started as a teacher, it took a toll on my idealism. I was teaching third-generation welfare recipients and learning of the historic downsides of this system, which often crippled people instead of helping them. While getting on their feet, individuals could be penalized with loss of payments if they worked too many hours, thwarting their ability to adequately use skills they acquired through programs like the one in which I taught. Many would return to welfare for support, since the pay wasn't enough to make up the difference. I could feel the frustration of the numerous fine women in my classes. I also understood that the system was too big for me to change—and I didn't want it to change me. With two years' experience behind me, I landed a new job at a vocational center in a public school district, which paid twice as much to teach three four-hour sessions of a class called Total Office Procedures (TOPS).

This school was designed to prepare students for the real world following high school, so the class was run like a model office. I fell in love with the students and spent many hours counseling them on the traumas of adolescence they were experiencing, as well as teaching them secretarial skills. I was twenty-four and an intuitive teacher as well as their enthusiastic champion, encouraging them and taking great pride in being their confidant. I never tired of listening to their stories and helping them find a way through their teenage chaos.

I was especially fond of one student named Kathy and was continuously challenged by her antics, which jeopardized her enrollment. She was a younger version of myself—alternately vulnerable and defiant, boisterous in public, sensitive in private. But with me, she talked openly about her fears and showed the devastation she felt upon receiving poor test scores, thinking herself stupid or incompetent. In the next breath, she would lash out about the absurdity of certain rules, trying to cover her exposed tenderness. One day, the assistant principal came to my class looking for her. When he told me she was on the verge of expulsion for driving her car to school, I explained that she was a rebellious kid, but a good one, and that she would probably disregard the rules and continue to drive for the last two weeks before graduation.

"You need to decide if you want to throw her out of school for this minor infraction, knowing she will probably never finish high school, or let it go," I told him. Bill looked at me, smiled and shook his head, and then left the room. Kathy graduated, and I was relieved that she had made it.

At one point, John, the principal, suggested that I spent too much time counseling the kids. Just days earlier, in moments of my own self-reflection, I had added up all the days I had been alive. It amounted to 8,766 days, if you counted four leap years. Then I tried to remember the times I felt most seen, alive, important, or encouraged, and each one had to do with the moment that someone took the time to really listen to me, to believe in my dreams, to take me seriously, or to build my confidence. I asked John to add up all the days he had been alive and to tell me what was important to him. If it was any different than my discovery, I would listen to his advice; otherwise, I was going to go on spending time talking to the kids. He never again asked me to change.

Living in a new town, I was removed from anyone who might have suspicions about me—no former college chums around, no high school friends who might have suspected that I was interested in women. Thoughts of Gina, Nicky, and Julie drifted farther away, and my fears about being gay subsided. I took more classes at Eastern Michigan University in the evening, where I discovered an appetite for learning that had been squelched in my working-class upbringing, where all the focus was on helping my brother succeed. While I had finally graduated from college, I had never applied myself in a rigorous way. Indoctrinated with the mindset that my brother was the "smart one" and I was the "creative one," I had little understanding of my true academic gifts. Taking graduate classes now, I felt intellectually challenged and discovered I had a talent for crafting thoughtful arguments. And positive feedback from my professors inspired me to greater aspirations. While my mother encouraged me to date more, I was content to spend time working on school assignments, creating lesson plans for my students, and enjoying the freedom of not being afraid.

Another Mike came into my life as a friend several months after I started work at the vocational center in the fall of 1973. He wasn't attractive to me—his scraggly brown hair drifted over the back of his collar and stuck out on the sides like wings. He had a thin moustache and scars from acne that marked his face like scattered buckshot. Though he wasn't fat, he would be considered plump, and when he wasn't wearing overalls, he dressed in ill-fitting, straight-legged cotton pants. Large round glasses with wire rims sat on the bridge of his nose, magnifying his eyes. Hanging out with him was harmless because there was no juice there; he wasn't appealing to me, and he was married.

We had a mutual zeal for teaching, however, and over time we found a philosophical connection that led to spending time together after class in fervent discussions. Our shared interests in education were amplified by a childlike joy in simple pleasures. One day I brought a kite to school, and we flew it over our lunch hour. The cloudless sky was a vibrant blue, and the kite bounced and twisted in the wind for our entire break. Everyone who went by wanted to fly it or comment about how it should be a box kite, or that it should be bigger, or that we needed stronger string. It was a study in the human tendency to try and make things better, rather than just enjoy them as they were. Hating to bring it down when the bell rang, we tied it to a tree in the courtyard, where it flew the remainder of the day.

When we left school that afternoon, it was still aloft, and we agreed to leave it tethered to the branch, promising to meet at six o'clock in the morning to see if it was still up. If it was, we would continue to fly it before class; if not, we would go out for breakfast. We both arrived in the parking lot at the same time and raced to the back of the building to see if it was still airborne. It was not. We found it on its side in the field behind the school, wounded in a crash landing, so we left it to rest in peace and went off to breakfast.

On occasion, we hosted joint "discussion days" with our classrooms—mine filled with young girls in the secretarial program and his filled with boys from the Greenhouse and Landscape program. We brought in guest speakers and invited them to have dialogues about the issues on their mind—marriage, politics, careers. We instigated games of red rover and tag on our lunch hours with the kids, who, resisting their desire to be cool, joined in the fun. Our creative spirits were enhanced by each other, and we grew close through our conscious rebellion against the stuffy standards held by most teachers—wanting to touch the kids in ways that would kindle their heartfelt passions, whatever they may be. I was becoming more aware of the feminist movement and took the bold step of cutting up the "Miss Anderson" sign outside my door and posted one reading "Ms. Anderson"—wanting young girls to have an alternative role model, in addition to the plethora of traditional ones that surrounded them. Inside my classroom office, I had another sign that read, "Cinderella is Dead."

Mike seemed to be more enlightened about women's rights than most males in his cohort, and he appreciated my radical nature. He was also more emotionally available than other men, and, before long, we were taking leisurely rides in his blue Chevy truck at the end of the school day. I usually sat by the window, but after a while he pulled me toward the middle of the bench seat and put his arm around me. Afternoons often drifted into evenings, and we'd have dinner together in some town away from the school, followed by a dessert of making out like teenagers in random parking lots until he had to go home.

Though I knew these escapades weren't aligned with my values, I rationalized my behavior with the fact that we weren't sleeping together. But we were definitely having an emotional affair. And since he was a man, surely this meant I was normal, relegating those fleeting experiences in college back to their place as mere explorations—experiments in finding myself. Even though we could not be together in public, our secret relationship allayed my internal anxieties about being gay. His creative mind and ease in conversation increased his physical attraction, and the person I once saw as average became beautiful in my eyes.

Summer was coming and I had planned a two-month trip to Europe with friends. Our relationship had deepened significantly in the past few months and we spent much of our free time together whenever he could get away. Though I had misgivings about traveling all summer, I hoped the time away would bring some clarity about where this relationship was going. It was getting harder to spend time with him knowing that it was always limited by circumstance rather than desire.

To lessen the agony of separation while I was gone, we devised a plan to stay in communication on my trip. Without the aid of technology, the only way to connect was through snail mail and the occasional pre-arranged phone call from a telegraph station in a town on our itinerary. I would send him postcards in code and he would send letters to the post offices on our route. Through mail we would determine times we could talk by phone. The clandestine nature of our proposed plan heightened the excitement of the trip and the anticipation of mail from him was as titillating as the prospect of seeing the opera Aida in Rome.

Early on, Mike had shared the difficulties in his marriage, and I was a sympathetic listener, never imagining that we would fall in love as we learned more about each other's defiant streaks and progressive views on education. While I don't think I was the initial cause of their marital problems, our growing fascination with each other definitely played a role in his marriage's demise. Eventually, Mike separated from his wife, and we were free to explore our relationship more fully. Once his divorce was final, he was the first man I ever slept with, and I was sure that he was the one I would one day marry.

To mark the significance of our relationship, I bought him a beautiful tiger eye ring. The stone shimmered in the light, anchored by a wide silver band that encircled his finger. He had always wanted a ring like that, and I was proud to give it to him.

As the following summer approached, we planned a six-week vacation out West together driving through Colorado to California, up the coast to Oregon and Seattle, then on to Vancouver and across Canada to Banff. He bought a new truck for the trip, and I stayed home to get everything ready while he went to his brother's wedding in Ohio. Since he was recently divorced, we didn't want to draw attention to ourselves. He didn't call me while he was on the road. Not expecting this silence, it made me uneasy, and I began making up reasons I hadn't heard from him—he couldn't remember my parents' phone number (where I was staying for the weekend), he was busy with the wedding party, there were no phone booths near the hotel.

He seemed distant upon his return but suggested we start our trip the next day, two days earlier than planned. I agreed, and we loaded up the truck, attached our bicycles to the bike rack, and took off west down I-94. It was a quiet ride to Chicago, where we found a small hotel outside the city to spend the night. The next day we rose early and drove straight through to Boulder. The conversation was strained, and Mike was unusually withdrawn. When I asked him what was wrong, he replied, "Nothing." His sister had recently died of a brain tumor, so I attributed his behavior to the grief he felt at her loss. We spent the night at my friend Sue's, and the next day he asked for a few days alone to hike in the mountains. Though the request made me feel even more unsettled, I agreed, and he left while I stayed in Boulder. Each day, I did something new to relieve my anxiety—bought paints, wrote poetry, and shopped for small gifts to give him when we reunited.

It was a long week before he called. Asking me to fly to meet him in El Paso, Texas, he reassured me that he was fine and that we would continue our trip west. I was so elated to hear from him, I didn't bother to ask how he had drifted over six hundred miles to the south when he had only wanted to spend time hiking in the Rockies. So, eager to be reunited, I bought the last plane ticket available—one-way, first class.

Exiting the jet way, I was greeted by smells of popcorn and barbecue. Neon signs for Bud Light, cowboy boots, and Stetsons competed for my attention. My eyes scanned the scene until I saw him walking around the corner. His stubbly beard, bloodshot eyes, and wrinkled denim shirt made him look like he had walked all the way to the airport. Instead of greeting me with open arms, he motioned for me to follow him to an empty sitting area. "Let's talk here," he said, when we were sufficiently removed from the crowd. "I have to tell you something." He averted his gaze as he spoke. That phrase never has a happy ending. My heart rate started to climb as I braced myself for what was next. "Some things have changed."

Well that seems evident, I thought. We had started a cross-country trip to California, up the coast to Banff and back down through Montana. Six fun weeks on the road camping out, hiking, and riding bikes. So far, we had made it to Boulder, Colorado, where I stayed while he went off to think in the mountains.

"I met someone at my brother's wedding right before we left," he continued. Now my heart was smashing into the walls of my chest. I reflected on our time apart. No wonder he hadn't called me. "I drove from Colorado to Alabama to see her. That is where I have been this past week. She is flying to L.A. to meet me."

I strained to grasp what he was saying as the airport spun in orbit behind him. He kept his head lowered, still avoiding eye contact. Finally, he looked up at me and said in a whisper, "I'm really sorry, Carol. I thought it best that I tell you in person." It was then I noticed that the tigereye was no longer on his finger.

You're sorry? I thought to myself. You have to be kidding. You asked me to pay for a one-way, first-class ticket from Boulder, Colorado, to El Paso, Texas, under the pretense of continuing our trip, where the only visible means of transportation I have now is a bicycle that is strapped to the bumper of your truck, and you are sorry? How stupid could I be? You're sorry, all right—a sorry son of a bitch. I'm sorry, too. Sorry I ever met you. Sorry I dated you when you were still married. Sorry I loaned you nine hundred dollars that I will probably never see again. And most of all, sorry I didn't listen to my mother.

My fingernails pressed into my palms as my fists tightened. The loudspeaker blared the final boarding call for a flight to Seattle. A little girl in a pink-and-white-checked dress twirled across the floor. I was spinning across the arc of my life.

"Do you want to fly home to Michigan?"

Actually, I wanted to fly to Mars or Jupiter, another planet, another universe, but home? Not really. Finally, I blurted out, "No, I don't want to fly home. I said I was going to California this summer, so drive me to California."

I forged ahead of him out of the airport, up the escalator two steps at a time, and down the wide hallway, hurled forward by an unseen force into the dusk of an El Paso sunset. There, he pointed toward his vehicle in the parking lot. I climbed into the back bed of the truck, and he got in behind the wheel. I lay down on the sticky plastic mattress, felt my cheek adhere to the blue synthetic surface as I rolled on my side, and curled up in the fetal position. I listened to the hum of the engine start as I stared out the side window. Feeling the shred of a breeze cross my face, I squeezed my eyes shut and bit my lip.

It was 1974, and a lot had changed since the perfect families of the fifties and sixties, when couples stayed together for decades. This was the year married persons in the United States experienced the highest divorce rate since the end of World War II. It hadn't occurred to me until this moment that if Mike would leave his wife for me, there was an equally good possibility that he might leave me for someone else.

We arrived at the airport in L.A. around 10:00 a.m., and Mike dropped me at the ticket counter, where I bought a one-way ticket to San Francisco. I left him standing there as I strode through the doors that led to my gate, past Dalton's Bookstore and the shoeshine stand, digging my heels into the tattered carpet splattered with ketchup stains. On my way to the gate, I found a phone booth, took a seat, and stared at the pattern of small holes on the metal partition. I reached out and touched the cool surface, pressed my forehead against the cubicle. Finally, I dialed my parents.

My mother answered. The silence on my end signaled something was wrong, and I could hear the panic in her voice as she kept asking, "Are you there?"

Without a simple place to start, I just blurted it out. "He left me, Mom."

She asked for details, and my story came out through intermittent sobs, along with my intense embarrassment at the stupidity of getting involved with a married man. I was hurt and angry—betrayed by a person I had deeply loved—tossed aside for someone he had known less than seventy-two hours. I had no one to blame but myself. I wished I had never met him, that I hadn't let myself fall in love, that I had listened to the warnings of my mother. My mom was kind and reassuring though clearly worried about my job, my future, and, most of all, my fractured heart. She urged me to come home, but I knew I couldn't. I promised to keep in touch every few days; then I hung up the phone.

I rented a car in San Francisco and found a small hotel on the coast, fifteen miles from the city. I spent my first week alone, wandering down by the wharf, eating cups full of bay shrimp, and visiting the tourist haunts, hiding my tear-streaked face with oversize sunglasses, trying to sort out what had happened. I wished for a shot of emotional novocaine to ease the wounding as I continued on my trip, bumming a ride up the coast to Portland, then Seattle, and then Vancouver.

I hit my lowest point after checking in at the YWCA in Seattle. I can still recall the faint smell of lavender as I walked the long corridor to my room, heels smacking on the tile floor. Opening the door to my room, I glimpsed a metal bunk bed with a plain white sheet and no spread; a large King James version of the Bible sat on a small end table marred by scratches and stains. A white basin with a rusted metal faucet and a tiny bar of soap in a fresh wrapper was on the sidewall. Hanging from the ceiling was a single light bulb without a shade. It looked like a fixture you might find over a pool table in a bar, only not as nice.

I sat on the bed and wondered if I would ever find love with anyone. I longed for home, for the comfort of my mother's arms around me, the reassuring words my father would say—that I was beautiful, smart, capable in every way. I longed for my own double bed, the soft light of my bedroom, the familiar objects that made me feel like I belonged somewhere. I curled up on the bed and fell asleep in my clothes with my boots still on. I awoke around 6:00 a.m., the overhead light shining in my eyes.

It was on that morning, after twenty-five days of being alone or in the periodic company of strangers of all stripes, that I hit a turning point. I realized that in addition to all the pain that had swallowed me on up this trip, I had also voyaged through to an unexpected yet dazzling clarity about my future. Those strangers, without knowing it, had helped me claim my dream of going to graduate school. Whenever I was asked what I did for a living, my standard response was, "I'm a teacher, but I always wanted to be a psychologist." I had repeated that response so automatically that I hadn't listened thoughtfully to my own words. Walking around Seattle my first morning, it was clear to me that I could do that now. I knew I didn't want to teach forever, and though I had been at this job only two years, I had saved nine thousand dollars—enough to pay for my tuition and an apartment my first year. The timeline was short from a practical point of view, but it was right on time for my heart, and I was aching for a change. I was making more money than either of my parents ever had, which was a great comfort to my mother. And though the thought of giving up that security for some unknown future employment was scary, it wasn't as frightening as staying in place.

Damn it. I would do it. I would leave my job, start over. The thought of telling my mother now seemed nearly as daunting as getting dumped in El Paso, so I quietly set about crafting a plan. First, I would find out options for psychology programs at Eastern Michigan University, where I had taken a few classes. Then I would talk to David Stokehouse about teaching part-time at the business school where I had been employed before. If things looked good, I would call John, the principal of my school, and resign. Then—and only then—I would call my mother.

I returned to San Francisco to spend a few days with a friend of my mother's and began to lay the groundwork. By mid-August I was ready to execute my plan and found a pay phone outside a convenience store across from my hotel. First, I called the admissions office at Eastern Michigan University and inquired about enrollment. Though I had taken a few classes there, I had never been formally admitted to a graduate program. I learned that they would not take me without a couple of undergraduate prerequisites I could complete there in the fall; then, I could apply in January for my specialist of arts degree in school psychology. But the admissions officer was clear: There was no guarantee I would get in. Scary news. What if I didn't pass statistics? I would be out of a great job and have no prospects for a new career. That stopped me for a moment as I weighed my choices, but I kept going.

My next call was to my old boss at the business school to see if he could hire me to teach part-time. He thought something might be available for the evening, come September, and he would keep me in mind. Then I called John Pollack, principal of the vocational center. My heart hammered a simultaneous tune of freedom and disaster as I waited for him to answer. Embarrassed by Mike's desertion, I felt awkward making the call, but John was kind and empathetic when I offered my resignation. He reminded me how much I loved the kids, what a great teacher I was, and how I had inspired him through many of our dialogues about education.

I had done it. There was no turning back now. I felt lighter, lifted by invisible wings and the prospect of fulfilling a dream. My final call was to my mother. I walked back and forth in front of the phone booth rehearsing what I would say, and then I went across the street to the drugstore and got a Coke. I scanned the shelves for some chocolate to bolster my resolve, then walked outside, picked up the phone, and dialed the number.

"Hi, honey," my mother said.

I reassured her that I was doing well and knew that I would be all right; we made small talk for about ten minutes. My throat tightened the closer it came to sharing the purpose of the call. When I couldn't delay any longer, I just spit it out. "I've done a lot of thinking, Mom, and I've decided that I want to go back to school." Not wanting to lose my nerve, I continued on before she could offer a challenge. "So—I quit my job and will start at Eastern in the fall." I told her of my conversation with David to return to work and assurances from the school that I could enroll in the two classes I needed as prerequisites. I stopped there and held my breath.

There was a long pause before she said, "Are you sure you want to do that?"

I responded with an emphatic "Yes!" and hoped my enthusiastic assertion would signal that the decision was made and not open for debate. I had called her last, fearing she would try to talk me out of it, but aside from modest objections, she didn't persist in protest. In spite of being brokenhearted and the fear I felt in taking this risk, I also felt confident that I would succeed. I did my best to reassure her that I knew what I was doing. The worry in her voice was not assuaged by my assertions. I knew the only thing that would convince her was the new job I hoped to have three years from now as a school psychologist.

While I still carried the wounds from Mike's abandonment, new waves of exhilaration seeped through the old pain at the prospect of returning to school. Now I had something to look forward to—a new goal for my professional life. If only I could gain the same clarity about relationships. My closest experience in creating anything akin to what my mother described between her and my dad had been with women. If I were ever to find real happiness, it seemed I needed to let go of all the old paradigms and expectations about who to love and how to love and find my own way.

chapter 11

women's libera-tion

I returned from my trip in September 1974, resumed my old job as a teacher at the Danbury School of Business, and enrolled in undergraduate statistics and experimental psychology at Eastern Michigan University. During the first semester, I lived in an apartment complex near my parents and spent most of my time teaching, studying, or going to class. Then I rented a room in an old sorority house in Ann Arbor for the winter semester. Though it was farther from both school and work, I had wanted to live there since I had dated a guy who attended the University of Michigan years before.

Thankfully, I passed Statistics and Experimental Psych and applied to the graduate program in School Psychology the same day I received notice. Living in Ann Arbor would make it easier to hang out with my new friends, Pat and Kathy, both of whom were Ann Arbor residents, and I was eager to spend more time with them. We all shared a rowdy streak that brought out the crazier part of each of us—in a good way. They also introduced me to many of the previously forbidden pleasures of life, starting with instructions on how to smoke dope.

"Move over," Pat said. "Here's how you do it." She sank into the couch next to me, leaned toward the coffee table, scooped up the finely crushed marijuana leaves, and spread them evenly in a narrow line at the edge of a small square of white tissue-thin paper. With one expert motion she rolled the whole thing into a perfect slender cylinder. "There—see how easy it is?" She pulled the joint to her lips, struck a match to the tip, and inhaled. The smoke swirled thick and pungent into the air as she forced what was in her mouth into her lungs. Handing it to me, she gestured for me to hold it up to my lips while she struck another match. This brought back memories of sitting with Gina on the picnic table in O'Shea Park the first time she offered me a Pall Mall cigarette. I knew better now than to suck on it like a straw; but I had never smoked dope before, so I handed it to Kathy to watch her technique before I took a toke. No one in my previous circles of friends smoked marijuana, and though I knew it existed, I had only a faint notion of the possible effects. None of how life was supposed to turn out had worked for me so far, and after my travels, little phased me about the secular world. I had no qualms about getting high with my new pals just to see what it was like.

Soon we were rolling on the floor in laughter, mocking Dr. Miesel, our psychopathology professor, who fancied himself to be a miniature Dr. Freud—dressed in his tweed jacket, vest, and gabardine pants, his beard finely manicured and cut close to his face. He was short with thinning hair he parted on the left, just like his idol, Sigmund. In class, he would strut back and forth in front of the room, his left hand on his hip, his wire-rimmed glasses balanced precariously on the end of his nose. If he could have smoked a cigar in class, I'm sure he would have.

Both Pat and Kathy were enrolled in the clinical psychology program but we had overlapping classes. Pat was in her late thirties with three kids aged seven to thirteen. Kathy was three years older than I and had a three-and-a-half-year-old daughter. Both were returning to school to follow a dream deferred. Though I didn't know it at the time, I was returning to school to find myself. Both Pat and Kathy were divorced and, like me, caught up in the excitement of the women's movement careening through the seventies like a kayaker sliding down a waterfall. Ann Arbor was famously a bastion of liberal activity spawned by student activists who championed change not only at the university but also in the city itself.

It was like moving to a new country compared to my sheltered life in Detroit just forty miles east. For many women, a fierce restlessness had been building for decades. And when Kate Millett, in her groundbreaking book *Sexual Politics*, articulated the oppression that women had experienced for generations, it unleashed a torrent of rebellious energy across the continent. The fact that her book sold eighty thousand copies in its first year, when one had to drive to a bookstore to get it, was an affirmation of how thirsty women were to hear a female version of the truth.

Pat was definitely into men, and Kathy was, too, hanging out with a political activist named Andrew. Both were becoming staunch feminists whose politics were on the far side of liberal, and we spent a lot of time talking about the articles in *Ms. Magazine* or the latest book on women's issues. One we read together was *Rubyfruit Jungle* by Rita Mae Brown—a fictional story about a self-possessed lesbian character who was strong-willed and brilliantly funny. The ease with which these topics were discussed created a comfort in me and a hunger to spend all my spare time with my new pals. I didn't know what I was anymore, but I began to feel that the "me" crafted by my family and the larger culture was not the authentic one. This environment enlivened my curiosity about everything—racial issues, women's rights, and, most especially, the possibility of loving women without persecuting myself. Here, I felt safe to begin exploring my attraction to women without the constancy of my internal judge hovering over me. Let Dr. Miesel have Freud; our heroines were Betty Friedan, Gloria Steinem, Germaine Greer, and Kate Millett—women who, in their intellectual treatises on patriarchy and the subjugation of women, were putting into words the things I had long felt.

When I wasn't teaching, the three of us hung out together, and I eagerly participated in the worldly education I had been denied the first twenty-six years of my life. We explored our new freedom as women, dressed in overalls and plaid shirts rather than skirts and blouses. We refused to wear makeup, to shave our legs, or to wear bras in protest of being viewed as sex objects among a sea of men who couldn't quite grasp why grown women, most often referred to as girls, felt oppressed. We attended workshops on women's health, participated in protests, and advocated for equal rights for women in school, at work, and in the home. My mother, who had been excited about my improved appearance after our weight-loss experiment when I was sixteen, judged these new developments as serious regressions. Whenever I appeared in my new attire, her exaggerated eye-rolling would be followed by familiar words: "Oh, Carol, can't you wear something else?"

A year passed, and Kathy and I became closer—spending more time as a pair, outside the trio we had formed. She was about my height with long, straight brown hair parted in the middle that hung past her shoulders, often hiding a portion of her face on both sides. She read and wrote poetry and had a vocabulary I envied. She asked piercing questions that made me think about patriarchy and the role religion had played for eons in the suppression of women. She was adamant about our rights as females and sought justice for all who suffered at the hands of patriarchal institutions. Kathy had no patience for those who were less intelligent or insightful than she, and that included most everyone in any room she occupied. She challenged me to think rigorously, to question the status quo on multiple fronts, and to take a public stand for the things I claimed to care about. She was a member of one of the few remaining chapters of Students for a Democratic Society (SDS), a radical activist movement in the United States.

I, myself, had grown agitated about inequality and injustice over the years, as my understanding of prejudice grew—heightened largely through exposure to the riots in Detroit in the late sixties and to the inequality women faced in the workforce. I experienced this directly too—most sharply right after graduation from Western, when my application for an entry-level position at Ford Motor Company was denied. I was outraged when the position was offered instead to a male student who graduated in my same class, while I was given the option of taking a secretarial position at half the pay and with no room for advancement. I was without allies or a way or place to focus my discontent in those years. Now I was surrounded by legions of like-minded women who dared to ask why things were the way they were and who were adept at providing arguments for why they shouldn't stay that way.

In the spring of 1975, Kathy, Pat, and I attended a psychology conference in Chicago—another first for me. It was a year and a half into my three-year program. After two days of intense workshops and speeches, Kathy and I opted to escape the planned sessions on the third day and go to the art museum instead. Taking off in the morning without sharing our plans with anyone, we wandered the streets of Chicago, our conversations occasionally drowned out by the rumble of the "L" train that lumbered overhead. As we perused the gallery's paintings and artifacts, I felt a familiar buzz when we accidently bumped into each other in passing or when her hand lingered slightly longer next to mine when I handed her a bottle of Pepsi. The racing pulse, the unanticipated flash of joy in being alone together, and the emerging self-consciousness were all signs that we were interested in more than the artwork. The day was filled with the sizzling enchantment that accompanies sexual attraction—each look or smile rich with subtle revelations.

It was emancipating to realize that these waves caused elation rather than drowning me in angst or shame. There was no brooding Reverend Mitchell chasing behind me, nor did I have the faint awareness that, were I to enjoy these feelings, a terrible punishment would descend upon me—that God would leap over the bridge above and strike me dead. I no longer thought I would go to hell for living in a body and enjoying the sensations that went with that. Because I'd been invited in the past year to scrutinize my own and others' beliefs through class assignments and discussions with friends, a slow but steady transformation had been unfolding. While I hadn't yet crafted a new paradigm about God and sin, I no longer held the cruel one to which I had been so bound.

Kathy drove on the ride home from Chicago. The juice of our connection flowed through the upholstery from the front seat to the back as I caught her eyes, again and again, seeking mine in the rearview mirror. We dropped Pat off at her house and then went back to Kathy's. She lived in an old neighborhood where large, shady maples and oaks with voluptuous canopies lined the street and moderately sized homes sat within yards of each other; gardens were showing signs of spring. Though it was May, there was still a chill in the air.

"Would you like to come in?" she asked. "I have one more night of freedom until my ex brings my daughter back." The house itself was built sometime in the forties or fifties, boasting the elegant charm that solid wood floors, curved archways, and plaster walls brought to even small homes built in that era. The living room was cold, and she asked if I would build a fire as she set about finding us something to eat.

Wadding up the *Ann Arbor News* into paper balls, I arranged them strategically on the grate in the fireplace and then set slender sticks of kindling to balance across them before adding medium-sized logs and finally the big ones. I opened the flue, struck a match, and touched it to each wad of paper. My well-designed and careful construction did not disappoint as I watched the dry twigs catch fire and the draft up the chimney ignite a frenzy of heat and light. Staring into the flames, I was reminded of Nicky and how she would light a match and watch it burn as she spoke. I could still feel the rush her gaze would cause—so close in spirit and so far from knowing how to nurture such a special love. I wondered what would have come of it had we met here now, six years later.

Kathy appeared from the kitchen with a plate of snacks and then disappeared into the bedroom, returning with an armful of blankets and pillows. We spread them out on the floor and put the plate between us. I wanted to both waltz and race into this moment as I felt a blend of calm and excitement. Kathy had never been with a woman. And though I had, it had never been without the attendant shame. A swell of shyness came upon us both as we studied the plate of food and avoided eye contact. In Chicago, we were most often in the presence of others. Even on our walk around town, we knew we would return to the group. It was fun to flirt, to get close to the edge, but now we were seated on it—and I wasn't sure if we would fly or fall.

In truth, we floated, lying in front of the fire, feeding each other apples with peanut butter, exchanging long gazes between bites and sips of wine. Kathy brought out a joint, and a few tokes brought a mellow vibe and ease to the conversation that went into the night—we elaborated further on tales of growing up in different social classes, she in Grosse Pointe, an affluent suburb, and I in Detroit, a working-class neighborhood. She came from wealth, I from modest means, her college education paid for before she was born, mine earned through summer jobs as a secretary. She grew up with a stay-at-home mom, I with a stay-at-home dad. Her father was an attorney, my mother a secretary. We were Mercury and Pluto in the distance between our formative realities, yet we were drawn by the powerful magic of attraction toward the sweetness of sensual pleasure in front of the fire all through the night.

I awakened feeling the physical pain of a cricked neck from sleeping all night on the floor but none of the old emotional pain I had suffered in the past when waking up next to a woman. Along with the sunlight spilling through the living room window was a delirious peacefulness that had eluded me for years, and we snuggled closer together, enjoying the freshness of the morning.

Kathy and I continued to include Pat in our escapades, and she was the first person we told of our night together and the feelings we had for each other. This time, I felt eager to share the news—proud to be with someone for whom I felt this budding love without the need to kill it before it had a chance to sprout. Ann Arbor was a place that made that possible, and Pat's liberal views made it safe.

Shortly after we met, Kathy moved into a cooperative house with two other women. Both of her housemates were jubilant gay women, proud of their sexual identity: Maureen was the lesbian advocate at the University of Michigan, and Theo was in a radical phase of life, living in opposition to anything that could be considered the status quo in America. She claimed to be a political lesbian, a term used to describe women who were not necessarily physically attracted to other women but who were in opposition to being dominated by the patriarchy. Being this kind of lesbian was a matter of principal. Choosing such a path was beyond my understanding, given I had fought so fervently to not be a lesbian of any kind.

Many fascinating women who were part of the cultural movement for change came through that house, bringing with them the most recent feminist articles and notices of female speakers scheduled to be in town in the coming weeks. Small groups of us would talk for hours about the need for equality in pay and employment and, above all, the need to have control over our own bodies.

The same deep emotional bond I had had with Nicky and Julie was available with many women here, with fewer constraints around physical expression. Even straight women acknowledged their attractions to other women in this new world of feminism, not fearing where such attractions might lead. An evening in the Power Center listening to a panel made up of Gloria Steinem, Alice Walker, and Kate Millett left me high for days. Their articulate and elegant arguments on behalf of women's freedom lifted me to greater consciousness and commitment to live my own life in tune with what was important to me. It began to make sense for women to fall in love with each other.

Also of great significance to me was the emergence of a new genre of music written and sung by lesbians on the recently launched Olivia Records label, founded to market women's music exclusively. One evening, a woman showed up at Kathy's house with a surprise. She reached into her back pocket and whipped out a cassette tape. Waving it in the air, she taunted,

"Guess what I have? Does anyone have a tape recorder?" We all scrambled around the house looking until someone reappeared with the device. She popped open the slot and slid the cassette inside, then smacked it down and pushed the play button. Even on this bootlegged version of the original record, the sound of Cris Williamson's voice was piercing and sweet. She was singing about my experience of being a woman—of loving a woman. Her voice went through me with the resonance that only music can bring—instruments playing in harmony carried her melodies across this thin strip of tape like an anthem I had longed to hear from the first moment Gina rolled over and put her arm around me when I was fifteen.

Sweet woman
Rising inside my glow
I think I'm missing you
Singin' to me them soft words
Take me to your secret
Letting me know
Take me in
You let it all go
Oh the warmth, surrounding me
This night, staring, staring at me . . .
A little passage of time
Till I hold you and you'll be mine
Sweet woman, rising so fine

Her affirmation of love for a woman was the psalm my heart had ached for. She sang with passion and tenderness—unapologetically. I couldn't stop playing the tape, allowing the words to sink beneath my skin, absorbed by my blood and bones, replacing the hymns of my youth with the songs of my future.

chapter 12

white lilacs for the soul

I continued my double duty of work and school through spring semester and into the fall. Generally upbeat and happy to see the students for my evening shorthand class, the heels of my black leather boots clicked against the shiny floor as I hustled to my room—a friendly warning that I was about to arrive. I turned the corner and heard the bustle of my pupils scrambling to find their seats, steno pads, and pens. The whispers slid to a hush as I came through the door. "Hi, everyone. How was your day?"

Jennie, a sassy Italian girl about eighteen years old, boasted, "I took dictation to *The Phil Donahue Show* today and got most of it. He is such a jerk. He hardly lets anyone talk before he butts in and says his two cents. If I was on his show, I'd . . ."

Before she could finish her story, David, the director of the school, came into the room and made an announcement. "Class is dismissed this evening." He was stern, though nothing in his voice revealed the reason for his abrupt entry. Had a water main broken? Was a storm brewing? A tornado? Had I done something wrong? Was I about to be fired?

He motioned me to follow. The click, click, click of my boot heels now sounded more ominous than friendly. When we reached his office, he gestured for me to sit down, folded his hands in front of him, and twisted his fingers back and forth across his knuckles. I stared at his face, waiting. "I am so sorry," he began, "your mother just called. Your father died this afternoon."

A prickly feeling began rising from my feet up my legs. "This can't be true. I just saw him four days ago at Sunday dinner, and he was fine."

David looked pale himself as he continued to fidget, glancing down at the desk and then briefly at me. "I've called Lorna to come and drive you to your mother's house," he said as he straightened the things on his desk and moved papers from one pile to the other. "I will follow in your car."

"What did she say?"

He looked up at me and spoke softly. "She said that he was lying on the couch when she got home from work. She noticed he wasn't moving, and as she looked closer, she could see that he was gone."

I stayed, frozen in the seat, as he went to see if Lorna had arrived—my eyes riveted on the overhang of the desk where I noticed the dust that had gathered since the cleaning crew had been there. Paper clips sat neatly in a clear glass bowl next to a tall black canister filled with pens engraved with Danbury School of Business. A gold-and-silver paperweight shaped in the form of a giraffe sat on a sheath of pink phone messages as though standing guard over them. The date was October 9, 1975. I was twenty-seven.

It was my second year of grad school, and I lived in a studio apartment near the University of Michigan campus. It was an improvement over the single room I had rented the previous year. Just the day before, I'd received mail from my mother—a five-dollar bill paper clipped to a small scrap of paper with her handwriting:

White lilacs for the soul.
   Love, Mom

It was her way of saying, "Do something nice for yourself," of acknowledging my hard work and tight budget. Later that evening, I had picked up the phone and dialed my parents' home. I was about to hang up when my father answered. My dad didn't like to talk on the phone, but that night he stayed on the line.

"So tell me how you are," he said.

"Well, Dad, if you really want to know."

He chuckled and said of course he really wanted to know.

I told him I got a C– on my test, which was a little depressing, given that I quit a great job to do this and that I was practically living in poverty. He was quiet for a moment as he gathered his thoughts.

Then he spoke. "You are the most determined person I know," he told me, and then he recounted the story of my resolute efforts in learning to ride a bike: how I had stayed out long after the sun had gone down, lining up against the curb and taking off repeatedly until I had mastered the art of balance. I could hear him chuckle as he spoke, and, with my mind's eye, I could see the laugh lines that always formed around his beautiful eyes when he shared stories about me as a little girl.

"You know, all of the challenges in life are just God's way of building character, and you've got what it takes to tackle anything."

He also reminded me that the same intense fortitude he saw in me as a young child was still present and that I didn't have to excel at everything, I just had to pass. I always felt relief sharing a problem with my dad because he never tried to fix me but would paint a larger picture of the situation and help me to focus my attention on what was really important.

"You always make me feel better because you believe in me. No one else does that like you," I told him.

By now I had garnered a truer picture of my father, more aware of the pain he must have felt because of his illness and inability to support his family and how he managed that frustration with grace and dignity.

"You know how much I love you, Carol. I wouldn't trade you for anything. I know we have had some bumps along the way, but I think we both have learned from that." I listened carefully, bolstered by his encouragement. "You know, you can do anything, be anything your heart desires."

I walked back and forth in my small apartment, feeling calmer as he spoke.

"I believe in you, and I love you completely."

"You're the best, Dad! I want you to know that I would choose you all over again if I had the chance. I hope you know how much I love you."

We talked a few more minutes about upcoming events and other mundane things. Then he said, "Goodbye, dear," and hung up the phone. I didn't know those would be the last words I would ever hear my father speak.

Dennis returned with Lorna, who sat down next to me and said how sorry she was that my dad had passed away. We filed out of the office, and I got into Lorna's car. We made the twenty-minute ride to my parent's house in silence—Lorna driving and me reading the neon signs on storefronts we passed, numbness setting in.

We arrived at about seven thirty, and I leapt up the steps. My mother greeted me at the door and flung her arms around me. "Oh, honey. You know your dad loved you so much." Then, the tears.

We sat in the living room with a few visiting friends, and she repeated what David had told me, how she found my dad on the couch. Everyone talked about what a great man he was, and after twenty minutes or so I got up to get a drink of water. Walking back to rejoin the group, I noticed a notepad on the half wall of the kitchen. Flipping the page over I saw the unique scrawl of my father's handwriting in large, barely legible script. The words read, "I love Mom and I love my family."

I called Kathy, and she came at once. My mother didn't know the extent of our involvement, but the circumstances easily lent themselves to a display of physical affection seen by outsiders as the genuine empathy any friend would offer another in this situation. We slept in the same bed in my mother's house, and I was allowed the comfort of her softness, sleeping through the night held in her loving embrace as the sorrow seeped out through tears and regret that my father had died without ever knowing the truth about me. There were many times I thought about telling my dad about my feelings for women and my fears that I might be gay. It was only now, at twenty-seven, that I was able to honestly explore this part of myself without triggering internal shame and anxiety. The time I needed to settle into this truth was only months in the making, and now it was too late.

The days before the funeral sped by. What I most remember was driving around in my little green Datsun listening to the Carpenters sing "The End of the World." Every time I turned on the radio, that song was playing. I didn't know how people could go to the bank or stop for gas or shop for groceries as though nothing had happened, when my life was being swept across an unfamiliar landscape like a hot-air balloon in a ferocious wind no longer tethered to the ground. My brother, in his attempt to make me face facts, insisted I look at my father in the casket. "You won't accept the reality that Dad is dead if you don't look," Jim kept saying.

His hand on my shoulder felt more like a vice than a comforting touch. Though he meant well, I was adamant to discard his advice. I didn't need to see my father lying in a wooden box to know he was gone. In my last memory of him, he was alive, standing on the front porch with my mother as they waved good-bye. *That* was the memory I wanted to keep, and I did. Despite my brother's insistence, I never viewed my father in his coffin.

Only family members were invited to the final viewing before the funeral service, leaving me without Kathy by my side. In addition to the visible pain of losing my father was the invisible pain of being alone in these moments. On the ride to the cemetery, I watched my sister-in-law slip her arm around my brother in a gesture of comfort as I stared ahead and clenched my teeth. At the chapel, family members sat in the front row in straight-backed chairs—my mother on my left and my brother on the right, his wife next to him. I stared straight ahead through the vast curved stained glass window. The music played, the minister spoke, the tears flowed. In the middle of the service I felt Kathy's hand lightly touch my back as she leaned forward from the seat behind.

Later that night, Kathy, Pat, and I convened at my apartment and smoked some weed. Lying on the floor beneath the ten-foot ceilings, a pillow under my head, I allowed my body to sink into the floor and my mind to surrender to the loss of control my father's death had created. Looking up, I felt the trace of his spirit present in the room and wondered if he could see the truth about me now—know my love for women, and if, wherever he was beyond the physical world, he loved me still, as he had every day of his life.

The day after his funeral, Kathy and I walked on the trails around the Botanical Gardens, mostly in silence—occasionally arm in arm, when no one else was in view. Leaves fell around us by the dozens, littering our trail with a carpet of gold, brown, and burgundy. I could see and feel the beauty of death in nature—how letting go was a part of life. The sky was a blue color you see only in travel brochures for Sedona, and the beauty of the day brought fleeting moments of acceptance of this natural cycle, only to be lost minutes later.

It was still hard to grasp that my dad was gone, that all I had left of him was in the past, and that he would never see me grow into the person he always felt I would become. I feared I would forget how his voice sounded, how his fingers felt when he ran them through my hair, my head in his lap, and how his face looked when he smiled at me.

My father's death hung over me like sheets atop furniture in a house no longer occupied. At night, I would hold his favorite shirts up to my face and breathe in his smell, nuzzle into the flannel ones, and clutch them to my chest as I fell asleep. Instead of taking notes in class, I carried on a review of my father's life, starting at the beginning of my first memory: the day he drove home in the brand-new 1951 blue Ford, walked by me on the driveway, and patted my head as he said, "Stay out of the sun so you don't get polio, pudding-head duffy."

At the age of four, I had witnessed the tragedy that caused his disability to unfold in the middle of the night. When he came home from the hospital, he was different, unable to care for himself or for me. I became his eyes and steered him around end tables, the couch, and the rocking chair like an ant guiding an elephant.

I recalled all the ways he was my champion at home. If I returned from school with As, he was elated. If I came home with Bs, he was delighted. If I showed up with Cs, he assumed something was wrong with the teacher. Even when we disagreed—about Nixon and Watergate, about Vietnam—he would respond to my fury by simply saying, "You know I don't agree with you, but I really admire your spunk."

He was on my side whatever the challenge, like the time, during my teens, that my friends and I got into a squirt-gun fight with some boys on Plymouth Road as we walked by the local shops. One of the boys picked up a rock and threw it, missing me but breaking the storefront window of the cleaners. The old woman at the counter called the police on me, who then came to our house and confronted my dad.

I remembered him telling off the police, shouting at them, "My daughter would never do something like that. You had better get your facts straight before you come around here saying things that aren't true." And later that day, I saw him on Plymouth Road looking for the person who called the cops. He could find his way, after years of practice, around the eight square blocks we called our neighborhood, but he could still be easily confused when looking for a particular store. He had been given a white cane by an organization that serviced the blind, and that, at least, warned others that he couldn't see well. I watched him walk up and down the street taking long determined strides and slapping his cane against the sidewalk. He'd stop abruptly, then make an about-face and walk in the other direction, take a few more steps, and then turn back the other way. I could see that he was muddled, and his usually calm face was stretched in anger and frustration. As I watched, I felt a range of emotions from glee to sorrow—overjoyed at his zeal to defend me and sad he couldn't execute that defense in a way that would protect me.

I recalled the surprise dinner I planned for my mother's

birthday with my first paycheck. I was sixteen and had saved my entire monthly earnings (working at $1.10 an hour for a clothing store) for this special evening. I chose Fox and Hounds, a swanky restaurant located in the lovely Detroit suburb of Bloomfield Hills. My father's usual congenial manner had started to unravel even before we reached the restaurant. He slouched on the passenger's side but kept quiet. Once seated, he complained about the bad lighting, criticized the menu choices, and groused about the uncomfortable chair.

Returning home after an agonizing dinner, I fled to my bedroom and slammed the door, certain I would never speak to him again. After several minutes, he knocked gently and asked if he could come in, his voice contrite. I can still see him as he sat on the bed, his eyes downcast. "Can you forgive your dad?" he said softly. Before waiting for an answer, he went on and told me how hard it was for him that he couldn't do things like that for his family. He leaned over and put his hand on my knee. "What you did tonight was really special, and I know that I spoiled it. I hope you will find it in your heart to forgive me." With that he looked up, and so did I. It was then that I saw the pain in his face. He got up from the bed and left the room, not expecting me to understand or give an answer in the moment.

My father gave me unconditional love while my mother offered continuous opportunities for improvement, yet he didn't let me get away with things. If he thought I was on the wrong path, he would let me know. Once, when giving me feedback about my inability to hear constructive criticism (which of course I met with a defensive attitude), he blurted out in exasperation, "You don't want anyone to talk to you unless they give you a compliment."

I laughed every time I remembered that line—it was so uncharacteristic of him.

At the end of the day, I would pull out the file of letters he had written me during college. Reading his words and conjuring his voice allowed me to imagine he was still alive.

> *My Dear Daughter Carol:*
>
> *It was such a thrill to talk with you for a few moments last night . . . I just don't know how to find the words to express how much I love you, and what a joy it is to hear from you. I know life isn't always easy . . . We are so happy that you are having fun as well as a few bumps along the way, but it seems it is how we meet the bumps that molds us. I couldn't begin to tell you how proud we are to have a Daughter that has what it takes, to think straight and the courage to be a leader and follow through regardless of what others think or say.*
>
> *So nice to have this chat with you . . .*
>
> *Loads of Love, Dad*

Occasionally, I visualized a scene of coming out to my father, in which I would see the kindness in his eyes as I spoke and hear the comforting tone of his voice in acknowledgement of my words. I imagined his arms embracing me and squeezing me tightly, showing with his actions that no matter what I did, no matter who I thought I was, I could never lose his love. It was through his death that I learned the profound meaning of regret—not for something I had done, but for what I had failed to do.

chapter 13

break-fast at big boys

I tried to imagine what it was like for my mother to have lost my dad. New dimensions of the pain emerged, her grief coming in spurts of unexpected anger that careened off the nearest bystander, usually me. On rare occasions, her outbursts were followed by tears, her lower lip quivering as she struggled to regain control. In his absence, I saw plainly how the steadfast bounty of my dad's love held us all together—my mother, brother, and me. Now we were all adrift floating in our individual pools of grief.

My mother had always been the visible rock in our family—working all day, taking care of my brother and me, ferrying us to golf and bowling lessons on the weekends, taking us on expeditions to the Cranbrook planetarium. She led Jim's Cub Scout and my Pioneer Girls troops. She borrowed money for vacations by the lake and managed to always celebrate my birthday in a special way. And she made it all look easy. After my father's death, I came to see that he was the quiet source of her apparent strength.

The only reaction to a death I had witnessed my mother exhibit before was when my grandmother died. Returning home from school one day, I found her standing in the kitchen, encircled in my father's arms, leaning into his chest. Her eyes were red from crying, and her usually well-coifed hair was radically askew. In my twelve years of life, I had never seen her weep. Even in this obvious state of sadness, she calmly turned her head toward me and in a quiet voice said, "Hi, honey, Grandma died today."

She was like that—so matter of fact, as though she were reporting that Stan the butcher was out of chicken breasts. It was just a fact. No drama—just one of many truths in life; Grandma was dead. In spite of the equanimity with which this announcement was made, I remember being anxious about the real impact of the news on her. My grandmother was a source of familial connection, something my mother prized, even if it was only symbolic.

I often wondered who this woman was, this loving presence who wrote heartfelt letters throughout my life, expressing a yearning for closeness, yet when I got too close, she skidded away. She reminded me of a snow globe after it has been shaken: You can see that through the haze of floating particles there is a beautiful scene inside, but you can't touch it, and you can never really get close enough to discern the intimate details of the figures. The harder you shake it, the more obscured it becomes, until you can't see anything.

Marianna Williams, my mother, was born on August 14, 1908, in Paducah, Kentucky. At the time of her birth, women didn't have the right to vote and, in many states, couldn't serve on juries, make contracts, or control their own earnings. Also, federal courts had ruled that the Fourteenth Amendment's guarantee of "equal protection of the laws" did not apply to women. Life expectancy for a female then was less than fifty-three years.

When I consider the cultural milieu into which my mother was born and how that template gave her a definition of herself as a child, and then a youth emerging into adulthood, I feel how her sense of possibility was squeezed into a container the size of a thimble, even before the personal trials of her own life disrupted the natural course of expectations laid out for women.

So I try to comprehend the emotional world of a smart little girl who grew up in the South with one older sister, a younger sister, and a baby brother. I try to imagine her shock at the unexpected death of her father when she was fifteen and why, in spite of her closeness to him, she rarely talked about him dying and never about the impact that had on her. She never said where she was when she heard the news; how she, her sisters, and her brother responded to the announcement; if anyone came to comfort them; or if her mother cried. Nor did she speak about the details of the funeral, what she thought about on the train ride to Kentucky where they buried him, who came to the service, or whether there were flowers. She didn't tell us where they stayed or what the minister said as they laid her father to rest. She never said how long it took her to get over it or if she ever had. I was sure that sure my grandmother had never recovered by the vacant look in her eyes and the invisible shield of protection she built around herself like a sheet of emotional plexiglass.

My mother also spoke sparingly of the experience of being shipped off to live with her aunt and uncle in Chicago for a year while she attended secretarial school. Noting a photo of her in her teens, I see a slim, willowy young girl standing straight as though at attention, her arms at her sides, curled fingers touching her dress that blows in the wind, unfurling like a flag flapping against her birdlike legs.

I think about this wispy adolescent being dropped off at the Michigan Central Train Station in Detroit two weeks after her father died to travel by herself to a foreign city to live with people she barely knew. She appears in my mind's eye entering the mammoth structure with vaulted ceilings and marble columns and massive chandeliers that hang in a line overhead through the center of the corridor like giant Christmas ornaments against a backdrop of stone etchings carved into the archways above. Row upon row of solid wood benches stretch the full length of the waiting area, like pews in a great cathedral, filled with passengers sitting in silence reading the *Detroit Free Press* or doing crossword puzzles instead of reading Bibles, oblivious to the grief and fear resting inside this young girl who sits alone, fingering the handle on her suitcase while waiting for her train to be called. Perhaps her eyes are focused on the enormous round clock that marks time above the ticket booths, everyone glancing toward it periodically, hopeful they haven't missed the call to board their train.

What could she have been thinking as she sat on the firm seat of the bench in the waiting area, dressed in her best clothes in early fall, as the chill of the Michigan air began to creep in through the open doors?

I can imagine it was then, as a teenager in Chicago, that my mother first learned to push her feelings away, to lock them up in a small invisible container and set them just outside her heart, where they couldn't run wild, tearing up her inner world like a bulldozer ravaging a virgin forest. Wherever it started, she nurtured a fierce kind of fortitude throughout her life that allowed her to endure the many hardships that ensued, while at the same time keeping me from knowing her more deeply. It was a territory that she adamantly refused to inhabit, just as it was the space I most fervently wished to explore.

Her father's death had catapulted her into the workforce. It was 1924 when she rejoined her family in Detroit, following her completion of school at the age of sixteen. She'd often recount the story of her first day searching for work, when her mother sent her out with a paper-bag lunch, a map of the city, and fare for the streetcar to find a job. This series of events marked the beginning of her transformation from a shy, introverted teenager into a plucky, resilient survivor—smart, sassy, and confident on the outside but still an elusive and complicated emotional being on the inside.

Years of forced independence and the need to survive on her own created a woman who personified contradictions. While her Southern, Christian upbringing taught her how to be gracious and polite in all sorts of company, her real-life experience in the world cultivated an unnerving sense of confidence that made others assume she was indomitable, in little need of support of any kind.

Beyond prompting me to be present more as a support to my mother, my dad's death was also a grave reminder of the fragility of life. I began inching closer to coming out to her, not wanting to make the same heartbreaking mistake of omission I had with my dad. We started a monthly ritual of meeting for breakfast at the Big Boy restaurant midway between our two houses. Entering the diner at our scheduled meeting time, several weeks after the funeral, I spotted her in our favorite booth and noticed how sad she looked, her hands folded in her lap, her eyes staring blankly ahead. This was new territory for me. It seemed that nothing could keep her down—not the death of her father at fifteen, not having to quit school to support her family, not living through the Great Depression on rationed gas and rationed nylons, not my father's disability of twenty-four years, not even her incessant worries about me. Looking back, I believe she was depressed, a concept I understood in theory but hadn't experienced personally, in the flesh—least of all with my mother.

I leaned down and kissed her on the cheek before sitting across from her.

"I spent the weekend at Hank and Bet's," she offered. These were her sister and brother-in-law who lived in a town fifty miles away. She talked of how my aunt became crabbier the longer she lived with my uncle.

On Saturday morning, Bet had barged into my mother's room, yelling at her, "Aren't you going to get up and eat with us? You know Henry needs to take care of his sugar." Her hovering, worrisome nature had been exacerbated by his diagnosis of diabetes years earlier.

"It hurt my feelings the way she screamed at me," she finally confessed.

It was unusual for my mother to share her feelings about anything, and I felt compassion for her as I sat up straighter in the booth and met her gaze. "I am so sorry, Mom. I can really understand how that must have made you feel. She used to be such a warm and generous person until she married him."

"I don't know what happened to her, but it's really kind of sad."

"What did you say to her?"

"Oh, I just ignored it and got up and made my own breakfast."

"Well, didn't you talk to her about it?"

While my mother was very direct when it came to settling an account at the bank or questioning a charge that didn't look right on a restaurant bill, when it had anything to do with family, she tended to avoid conflict. Instead of answering my question, she turned toward the window and said, "Oh, look. It's snowing outside. Isn't it beautiful?"

"Mom, we're not talking about the snow," I said in the calmest voice I could manage. "We were talking about how Aunt Bet hurt your feelings."

She turned toward me and said, "Tell me more about you, honey. What did you do over the weekend?"

Exasperated, my empathy rapidly slipped out of reach. I replied, "Oh—I forgot, we don't talk about feelings in our family. We look out the window and talk about the snow. We talk about what's for dinner or where we bought our shoes."

"Oh, Carol, don't get so emotional. What did you do over the weekend?"

Experience said this was a battle I couldn't win. While many of my mother's letters suggested she desired depth in conversations, our definitions of meaningfulness differed broadly, and while she could talk about the prospect of such closeness in writing, it was almost impossible to achieve it in real time. She would divulge a morsel of information about a feeling and then immediately drop into superficial conversation, as if she had said nothing of importance.

Silently, I chided myself: You can do this. You are pursuing a graduate degree in psychology. You have traveled across Europe for two months by rail with only a backpack. You were dumped in California by your boyfriend and survived. Surely you can go for half an hour and talk about nothing with your mother.

I finally told her I had gone to see Nanci Griffith at the Ark, a local music venue. Dismayed by my inability to engage her in meaningful dialogue, I walked off to the buffet to pile cubes of cantaloupe and strawberries, extra-crispy strips of bacon, and a dollop of eggs onto a plain white plate. As I rounded it off with a half piece of well-done rye toast, a familiar heat crept up my spine; an old pressure weighed on my chest. I pierced a few grapes with my fork and piled them on top of everything, as though I could kill the feeling inside by attacking fruit with silverware.

I sat back down at the table, where my mother continued her surface talk. "I love the way they make their eggs here—just the right amount of butter with a dash of pepper."

This determined equanimity had been her fallback all her life. What did it cost her to keep it up? What would fall apart and what would be born, for her and for me, if she ever let it go? I pressed. "I know you don't want to speak to Bet, but let's just imagine—if you were going to, what would you say? I'm curious."

"I don't know."

You've got to be kidding, I thought to myself. So connected was I to my internal panorama of feelings that it was hard to imagine she didn't know *anything* about hers. I pushed the soggy eggs around my plate with my unbuttered toast and waited for her to respond. Instead of playing the make-believe game I had offered, she countered with, "What do your friends think of you and all your questions?"

I thought carefully before responding, "I think my friends actually love me and chose me as a friend because of my curiosity and interest in their lives. My questions make them feel cared for." I didn't go into my further belief that she too had chosen me, long before my birth, and that in my emerging cosmology, it made sense that, from the vast array of souls available to incarnate into her womb, she was involved in the selection. That point, I kept to myself. "Furthermore, getting to what's important for people and seeing beyond the surface is what made me successful as a teacher and will hopefully make me a great psychologist."

She shook her head and twisted uncomfortably on the vinyl bench. "I don't know, honey. I think you should just let some things be."

I sat there and watched the snow falling outside, just as she'd invited me to. I felt helpless against the perennial wall separating me from her. I looked at her again. The overhead lamp muted her features—her beautiful hands, the way she balanced toast between her fingers, and how her polished nails always matched her lipstick. She was searching my face for comfort, acceptance, for simple presence. I remember our conversation unfolding like this:

Everything in me softened before I spoke, my sarcastic tone replaced with a loving voice. "It's like this, Mom. Let's say that you're kind of an artist, and one of your gifts is to help people see things more clearly or to help them believe in themselves. Everywhere you go, your friends and coworkers appreciate and love your art—they write you thank-you letters and comment on your insight and wisdom—they ask you to share your art with other friends or colleagues because they see value in what you offer. And the one place you would like your art to hang is in your mother's house. And even though she loves the artist, she just doesn't like that kind of art."

She seemed to be considering what I had said, and I waited for her to speak. I no longer felt the need to push her to respond in some way that was important to me. Finally, she said, "It's not that I don't like it. It's just that it's too painful."

I understood something in those words I had never fully grasped before. For many years, I thought my mother just didn't want to talk about anything that would reveal her true feelings—as though it wasn't normal for people to be angry or disappointed or hurt by the everyday experiences of life. Because she spoke so matter-of-factly about her early years, without revealing the pain she'd endured, I had grossly underestimated the immensity of grief she had covered up for decades, as a means to survive her many losses. And though her words were hard for me to hear, I knew they were true, and I was deeply grateful she'd helped me see this profound reality.

I had intended at this breakfast to come out to her. Clearly she wasn't ready for that conversation—nor was I.

chapter 14

finding freedom

I t had been two years since my father died, and I had graduated and become a school psychologist in the town where
my mother lived, making it easy for me to stop by on my
lunch hour or pop in after work. My relationship with Kathy,
while brief, was the beginning of finding my identity as a gay
woman. I was not alone in this arena, as many people (gay and
straight alike) were investigating all kinds of sexual freedom,
getting away from rigid and oppressive attitudes about sex—a
long-lasting gift from the Puritans. It was a stimulating and
refreshing time for those bold enough to plunge into the
experimental fray.

I started attending women's dances at Canterbury House in
Ann Arbor, where I met lesbians of all types and sizes dressed
in many different styles. Gone were images of butch and fem,
replaced by a plethora of real-life alternatives. There were
women like me—committed to professional careers, intelligent,
and fun loving; there were women who inspired and challenged
me with vibrant discussions about politics and women's roles
in the world. More important than their being gay, these were

feminists who wanted to make a difference through taking on roles beyond that of being a mother, a housewife, a secretary, or a teacher. Not that those weren't noble pursuits when chosen by the women themselves, rather than imposed or prescribed by men, who, until now, had set the standards for what women should do and who they could be.

I had also returned to my love of athletics and joined a women's softball team sponsored by the Blind Pig, a local bar in town. This early summer day, I was recovering from a pulled muscle in my leg, injured during practice the night before. Linda, one of my teammates, had dropped off a heating pad at my apartment afterward and was stopping by this evening to pick it up. I was a little surprised she had gone to the trouble, since we didn't know each other well, but I opened the door and invited her in for a drink. It was a reasonable gesture, since she had come all the way across town to check on me. We sat on the floor in my small living room, leaning up against pillows, a bottle of wine between us. After a few minutes of small talk, she got right to the point. "I've been watching you play ball for the last two years, and I've always been attracted to you."

I choked on my wine, and my eyes widened—had I heard her correctly?

She continued, "You know, I've never been with a woman, and I might get nauseous if you kissed me, but I would really like to go out with you."

Gulping my wine now, I was shocked and intrigued. "But I thought you were married," I said, though the look on my face alone must have expressed my confusion.

"I am, but my husband and I have an open marriage."

It was 1977, and open marriage was one of the latest fads for heterosexual couples. I slugged down the rest of my wine and looked at her with an amused smile. "Okay, back up a little bit here. What exactly do you mean by 'open'?" I poured another glass of wine for myself as she went on.

"We are free to sleep with anyone we want as long as we tell each other in advance. If either of us is available when the other is, we get first choice to spend time together."

"It seems like being sexually involved with other people would cause a lot of jealousy." Certain I would never want a relationship so open, it was hard to imagine how two people could navigate such emotional complexity.

"Sometimes it does, but we have been able to work that out."

"Wow," was about all I could manage.

Of the numerous opening lines I'd ever heard from either a man or a woman, this was the most memorable and hilarious. I didn't know whether to laugh or kiss her on the spot to find out what her reaction would be

In the last two years, I had found people who were open and proud of their lifestyles, whatever they were. This had nurtured a sense of normalcy in me. While I was not prepared to "come out" to the world, I had at least come out to myself and a few close friends, leaving the judgment and damnation of the Baptist church far behind in favor of a more benevolent spiritual path of my own design. I felt increasingly connected to the Divine through nature and found greater peace on a walk in the woods than in a church of any kind. The beauty of the world around me became my cathedral, and it was easy to marvel at the grandeur of the stars without the need to attribute their creation to God. Best of all, nature accepted the reverence I offered without judgment.

While I had been successful in attracting men and had even fallen in love with a few, I was often reminded by my mother that I should defer to them, be less intense or demanding. I also found that many men of my generation agreed with her proposition and were caught by surprise with the new demands made by feminists who wanted equality. Even if a few men favored these shifts, they were without much-needed support in learning how to navigate a world where partnership took precedence over patriarchy. With women, I felt my strength and independence were assets—traits most women found attractive. I could be strong or vulnerable, or both, as the situation required. There was no set role for me, no limited female part to play, and this created greater room for self-discovery.

Linda was the most recent of several romantic pursuers since I started attending dances and playing softball. I seemed to be going through a kind of gay adolescence, discovering myself attractive on multiple levels to the women around me in ways and on a scale that had never happened with men. So hungry for physical connection after years of stuffing away my emotional and sexual feelings for women, it was like unleashing a spring-loaded can of confetti. I was easily seduced by them all, and Linda was the most unforgettable.

She stayed for another drink, and we continued to talk—about our upbringings, our parents and siblings, and members of the softball team. I hadn't paid much attention to Linda before because I knew she was straight. This night, I noticed she was quite attractive in both appearance and energy: her mid-length brown hair, parted on the left, curled in a wayward fashion; her blue eyes focused on me felt inviting; and her wide smile revealed a small dimple in her cheek, suggesting a penchant for mischief. She was tall and slender and looked striking in her pressed shorts and checkered shirt. More than anything, I appreciated her flat-out, no-holds-barred, unabashed honesty. It was evident she knew what she wanted and wasn't afraid to go after it. "So what do you think about going out?" she asked as she got up off the floor and picked up her car keys.

Given her explanation about her agreement with her

husband, her invitation seemed harmless. Everything was out in the open. No one was lying about anything, so there was nothing to feel guilty about. "Why not?" I said, bemused by the whole encounter. We hugged goodbye and promised to meet the following Thursday for dinner. Meanwhile, I spent a different night with each of the other women in my new romantic orbit, grateful for the summer vacation afforded by my new job as a school psychologist; I wouldn't otherwise have had enough time to fit in all my paramours.

Over the next two months, Linda and I spent countless hours together. It turned out that kissing me didn't make her nauseous at all, and our emotional closeness led to a fiery sexual attraction that was both sweet and raucous—creating the insistent desire to be together all of the time. Because her husband was a surgery resident on-call around the clock, she had significant time available. We went out to dinner, hung out with her children at the park, and shared picnics and canoeing trips down the Huron River. I should have been more attuned to the danger such a liaison posed, after my experience with Mike; but I was living in the moment and didn't want to pay attention.

Later that summer, Linda took me to her high school reunion in Muskegon and to meet her parents on their farm there—all in the guise of friendship. Linda had been a star in high school— the straight-A student, co-valedictorian, the gregarious and charming head of her class. Being married and having children was a great cover. No one would suspect that instead of bringing a casual friend along to this gathering, she had actually brought her lover. After the social events, we shimmied down the sandy hillside of her parents' beachside property on Lake Michigan and built a fire in the sand. Listening to the water lap the shore and watching the moon rise over the lake, spreading a beam of light as far as we could see, was intoxicating. We lay down on the ground together and felt the weight of our bodies press into the earth, eyes revealing a new level of connection.

Something changed on that trip, and by the time we returned from Muskegon, it was clear we had crossed into fresh territory. It was a space rich with new thrills yet fraught with familiar haunts, including the longing to be with someone I loved though society said I shouldn't—not because she was a woman, but because she was married, and in spite of the few couples exploring open marriages, it wasn't the norm. New pains, too, accompanied this deeper longing. We would make plans for dinner only to have them cancelled at the last minute because Joe was off of his shift at the hospital and wanted to spend time with her. They would head out on a family vacation, leaving me alone to wonder if she was sleeping with him. Why wouldn't she be? They were married. But I wasn't sleeping with anyone else—I had no desire to—and I hoped that even if she were sleeping with her husband, it only increased her desire to be waking up next to me.

Soon we were having long conversations by phone when she couldn't get away, and I started feeling the same agony I had felt with Mike while he was still married. I was repeating the same pattern, only with a woman. Despite their open relationship, the above-board announcement, and clear guidelines, Linda and Joe had no protection against forming deep attachments with outsiders. They had no formal way to agree not to fall in love with someone else, and, by September, it was clear that Linda and I had jumped off that emotional precipice and were in free fall.

I was grateful to return to work and get involved with projects that would require my full attention. I knew it was time to let go of this relationship, so, one night, with a weary heart, I broached the subject. We were lying on the floor by the fireplace in my apartment. She had on jeans, and her long legs stretched out across the cream-colored rug in a casual pose made her look especially beautiful. I fingered a glass of chardonnay and took a long, slow sip before speaking.

"As much as it pains me, I think it is time for us to stop this. It's just too excruciating," I said. She looked at me, her face soft in the reflected light. It was hard to go on, but I knew I had to. "It's has become unbearable for me, when you have to leave at the end of every day we spend together." I knew what I was getting into when this started, but neither one of us ever expected it would grow into what it had.

Her hair fell over one eye, and, in that moment, as she reached up and pushed the brown strands over her ear, she reminded me of Nicky. "It's not the way I want it to be," she finally said as she moved closer and took my hand.

"I don't think there is any other way," I replied.

She laced her fingers with mine and asked me to look at her. "For the first time in my life, I can imagine a partnership of equality—where there is a deep emotional intimacy, where both people take responsibility for the household chores, and childcare, and all the other things that require attention in life. I never thought it could be like this."

I was perplexed. I didn't imagine her ever leaving Joe; I didn't necessarily want her to because that didn't seem right. It wasn't part of the original agreement. I simply couldn't go on, craving something I could never have. "What are you trying to say?" I asked.

"I told Joe this morning that I wanted a trial separation."

"You did what?" My eyes widened in shock as my body absorbed the gravity of her statement.

"I love you, and I want us to be together," she said.

I raised my glass of wine to my lips and took a long slow sip, as though that would keep my heart from pounding ferociously. Had I heard her correctly? I was figuring out my response as the oaky taste of the chardonnay circled inside my mouth.

"I want that, too," I finally said softly, racked by the realization of what such wanting had led to. This whole thing had begun as an innocent lark—sparked by her admission of attraction to me. I would never have pursued a married woman. And, as she explained it to me, open marriage seemed like such a mature thing—civilized even, with partners able to explore their sexuality with others without risk to their primary relationship. In retrospect it seemed like an insane proposition and quite uncivilized. In this moment I saw the naïveté with which I had embarked on this engagement with her and the real threat it presented to their relationship—and to me.

Linda stayed a little while longer, and we lay in front of the fire imagining that one day we might be together permanently and she would no longer have to get up and leave at the end of the night. As we rested in silence, we were both aware of what a leap this would be—excited and terrified at the prospect as we held tightly to each other.

I lay awake for a long time after she left, wondering if she and Joe had an open marriage because they weren't happy with each other and it was a way to keep things interesting. I wondered if I had just happened along at the right time or if I was personally responsible for their potential breakup. If it hadn't been me, would it have been someone else? What impact would this have on her children? I wondered if Linda would really go through with it. Half the time, I was giddy at the possibility, and the other half, I was overwhelmed with fear that she really would.

chapter 15

who wants to be normal?

inda and I moved forward with many serious conversations about the viability of living together over the next month. And with each discussion, the reality shifted from what initially seemed like a wild and crazy idea to forming a concrete plan of action. Included in that progression was the looming need for me to come out to my mother. Because Molly and Sara were so young (eighteen months and three years) and not the least bit aware of the stir that would rise were people to find out that their mother and I were more than friends, I was quite sure that if I didn't tell my mother first that I was gay, they were likely to. Perhaps Sara would blurt out this truth in the middle of Easter dinner at Aunt Gladys's house. Somewhere between, "What did the Easter Bunny bring you?" and, "Please pass the potato salad," she would announce that her father had said her mother was a lesbian. Or maybe Molly would share that I spent the night at their house in her mother's bed. It would come out innocently, in ways only children could express. No. That was not the way I wanted it to happen. I was going to tell my mother in private, before a three-year-old did it for me in public.

My mother and I were sitting in her kitchen after returning from the matinee performance of *Hello Dolly* at the Fisher Theater. I had always regretted not telling my dad, and if I were to have an authentic relationship with my mom going forward, I had to tell her the truth. Being with Linda amplified the necessity. I was determined that today was the day.

She put the teakettle on to boil, filled a plate with Russian teacakes, and sat down. Conversation turned to the usual topics. My brother and his wife were doing well in North Dakota. He was teaching chemistry at the university there. The weather was freezing, but they seemed to like it. I could feel my resolve slipping away with the tedium of trivial news, but then the conversation took an unexpected turn.

"Have you seen the news lately with all this talk about gay rights?" she said. "There was a big march in San Francisco on TV again just last week."

I clutched the sides of my chair, my teeth clenched. Was my mother really bringing up a conversation about being gay? Was she channeling my thoughts? I had been rehearsing opening lines throughout the week to talk about the subject, all of which slid beyond my reach with the shock of her query. "Sorry, what did you say?" I responded. She repeated her comment about the gay march on TV.

"What about that bothers you, Mom?"

It seemed the teakettle was screaming rather than whistling as I got up from the table and removed it from the stove. I poured cups of hot water for us and tried to remember the news of last week. Anita Bryant had been in the media for months, using a "Save Our Children" program to disguise a gay-bashing crusade—all in the name of God and Christian values.

Oh great, I thought, not the right moment for this conversation. But when would there be? I stalled further and asked another question. "Is this about Anita Bryant? And do you really think she is acting like a Christian?" I knew my tone was derisive, as I found it difficult to hide my cynicism regarding the hypocrisy of Christians who behaved in hateful ways that were anything but Christlike. I planted my feet on the floor and tried to get grounded.

I had brought Linda to meet my mother several months earlier, and my mother was fond of her, easily engaged by her intelligence and sense of humor. My mom's hope, of course, was that Linda's surgeon husband would introduce me to a doctor with whom I would fall in love. She hadn't counted on Linda falling in love with me, leaving her surgeon husband, and creating an instant new family with her two little girls and me. Coming out is hard enough, but if you have to tell your mother that you were pursued by a married woman with two children who was willing to leave a soon-to-be wealthy husband to spend her life with you—well, that would be hard for your best friend to grasp, let alone your sixty-nine-year-old mother reared in the Southern Baptist church.

"Well, I don't know," my mother said after a long pause. I could tell she was trying to decide if Anita's actions were Christian or not. "I just don't know why they have to hang all over each other in public."

I wanted to focus on something else—anything else—but if I was ever going to do this, I had to keep going. "Why shouldn't they be allowed to express affection in public?" I asked, trying to keep the tremor out of my voice. I went to the refrigerator and scanned the shelves. There was week-old macaroni and cheese, broccoli salad overcome by mayonnaise, and a plastic bag filled with sliced turkey. I wasn't really hungry, so I sat back down, my eyes fixed on the crystal salt and pepper shakers and the frayed cream-colored tablecloth that my parents had had for fifteen years. I noticed the faded stain of the red spaghetti sauce that I had spilled on it during the celebratory dinner to christen their new home.

"Well, it's just not normal."

"According to whom?" I shot back. Hearing the defensiveness in my voice, I reminded myself to stay calm.

"Oh, Carol . . . you know what I mean."

"Actually, *normal* just means that is what most people are doing. It doesn't necessarily mean that being normal is right or even the best course of action. It just means that most everyone agrees with that perspective."

I wanted to scream out, Who wants to be normal? Walk around a shopping mall sometime; you will see men and women with vacant-looking eyes schlepping large bags of material goods out to their Chevrolets. You will see lines of folks at the drive-through McDonald's eating greasy fries and burgers that will lead to triple bypass surgery by the time they're thirty. Normal is countries fighting wars over religious perspectives—killing each other in the name of God. Normal is mostly not thinking, not questioning, not wondering about anything. Even if I weren't a lesbian, I wouldn't want to be normal.

"Well, what do you think about it?" she asked.

My palms were sticky with sweat now, and my throat was contracted. The smell of Constant Comment brewing in my cup floated into the air. The patterned dots on the linoleum became three-dimensional and seemed to fade in and out of the floor. I looked at my mother, her hand on her teacup lifted to take a sip. I wished my father were here so I could look into his reassuring eyes, take his hands in mine, tell him how happy I was—explain that being gay didn't really change who I was as a person, that I still loved them and wanted them to love me. I knew he would understand. I wasn't so sure about my mother. But my father wasn't here now, and I could wait no longer, so I finally just blurted out, "Well, maybe I can tell you why they are marching in the streets, Mom. I'm gay."

There, I had said it aloud, or perhaps it said itself. It was hard to tell. Now it was hanging out there along with my fear and anxiety in the protracted hush that followed. I couldn't tell who was more surprised—she or I. So much for choosing the right words, rehearsing reasonable-sounding opening lines, and practicing to get it perfect. My eyes returned to the tablecloth; the red spaghetti spot loomed larger, more grotesque in the quiet. I could feel the pattern woven into the cloth with the tips of my fingers that moved back and forth in slow motion while I waited for her to speak.

"What about Harvey Colombo?" she finally responded.

I looked up, flabbergasted. Harvey was a guy I had dated for several months four years ago. My mother never really took to him and told me one day that she didn't think he was marriage material because not only was he Catholic but he also wore jeans torn at the knees, smoked cigarettes, and had a beard. Definitely not someone she had in mind for a son-in-law.

"Harvey? You never liked him and discouraged me from dating him."

"I know, but maybe that was wrong. You were crazy about him."

She got up and added some date cookies to the Russian tea-cakes and looked for the milk in the fridge.

"How do you know that you are gay? Maybe you just haven't met the right man."

Well, that's for sure, I thought to myself. For me, the right man was a *wo-man*. Better not lead with that. I hadn't given much thought to my second line, only the pronouncement. How could I possibly explain this to her? Her shoulders were hunched over, her face turned toward the wall. I hated trying to defend myself, but I knew how I answered this question would either end the conversation permanently or create room for future dialogue. My voice grew tender as I searched for words. "First of all, it's very hard to tell you this truth about me. But I realized after Dad died that not telling him had been a mistake. I want you to love me for who I really am, not for who you want me to be."

"I know. Your dad was always supportive of you—it's just harder for me."

"Losing Dad erased the fantasy that you would live forever. I was afraid that if I didn't tell you, there would always be something between us."

An eerie stillness filled the kitchen once more. The sun had set long ago, and the darkness nestled close to the house. Only the fixture over the table was on, its light bouncing off the speckled linoleum. I looked over at my mother, her hands resting on the table. She looked older since my father had died; a sadness had settled into her face in the last two years, and her usual optimism had been replaced by a dour presence. She had become someone unfamiliar to me, making me uncertain about what to do next. I wondered how this would change my relationship with her—whether she would ever speak to me again. I counted the blue and white tiles that were part of the backsplash for the sink and noticed that the trim on the window needed painting.

"Are you with someone?" she ventured.

I took another deep breath. "Yes. I met someone last summer. She is really an amazing person. You have actually met her and liked her."

I could tell as she wrinkled her forehead that she was struggling to imagine who it might be. I had not brought many of my friends around in the last few months.

"You remember Linda?"

"You don't mean . . ."

I could see her trying to compute things in her mind that didn't add up—her head tilted to one side, her eyes squinting. "Yes," I said. "I was as surprised as you are. Linda told me that she used to watch me play softball, and then she got on the team this year. I had no idea. One day after practice, she approached me about going out. She said that she and her husband had an open marriage and that she didn't know what it might be like to be with a woman, but she was open and interested."

My mother got up and unlocked the sliding glass door to let some air in. The cool breeze was a relief to us both. "I thought it was a fairly harmless idea, given that her husband knew about it and that they had had relationships with others during the course of their marriage. I wasn't expecting anything big to happen—but then we fell in love."

I didn't know whether to stop or keep going. I didn't want her to think that I had broken up a marriage or that I had even started the adventure. Somehow convincing her of my integrity in this situation was a bit of a stretch. Perhaps I had said enough and I should let this sink in before going on.

I heard her let out a big sigh as she stared into her cup. Without looking up, she spoke. "Aunt Noreen wrote me a letter after you and Julie went to visit her when you were twenty-two. She told me that she thought you were a lesbian and that I should encourage you to marry Mike."

It was my turn to be shocked. For eight years my mother had kept this secret from me. I had wondered why things had been so strained between my Aunt Noreen and me when I went to visit her in Tennessee with Julie—why I had had such a miserable time at her house, why she had been so cruel. I wondered who else might have said something to my mother that she never shared with me.

"I was so furious at her for saying that that I ripped up the letter and never spoke to her again."

I was so astonished by this revelation I could hardly form a thought in response. Was she enraged at the possibility it was true, or was she angry in defense of me? I didn't want to ask. "Why didn't you ever tell me?"

"I don't know. I was really peeved at her for saying it. I guess I didn't know how to talk about it."

All this time I was keeping a secret from her, and she was keeping a secret from me. Well, that explained why my mother had not been as friendly to Julie as she had been with Nicky. The only difference was that she had no suspicions about the latter friendship, and there was no need to tell her now. We sat in silence for several minutes, each of us absorbing the secret once held by the other. Finally my mother spoke.

"I need some time to think about this," my mother said.

"I know. I need a little time myself."

I got up and turned on the light in the living room so that I could find my coat in the closet. The relief of speaking was equaled only by the fear of the consequences. I stepped toward my mother and put my arms around her to hug her goodbye. With a kiss on the cheek, I turned and walked out the door.

My mind kept replaying the conversation in my head on the way back to Ann Arbor, and I wondered if my aunt's revelation in her letter had confirmed something my mother had long suspected or if it had never occurred to her that I might be gay. I also pondered the ways in which her secret about Aunt Noreen's letter had kept a barrier between us—imagining she was just as afraid to lose my love by addressing something that might not be true as I was of telling her something that was.

Days went by and my mother didn't call, even though we often spoke two or three times a week. It seemed I had lost both my parents—one to death and the other to overwhelming disappointment. Finally, midway through the third week, she phoned.

"Hi, honey," she said. "I have done a lot of thinking about our conversation, and I want you and Linda to come over and talk. I don't expect that I will change your mind or that you will change mine, but I don't want to live in fear of something that I don't understand."

I could hardly believe my ears. I was so proud of my mother for her courage. I was proud of myself, too, for following through with my revelation. This was certainly a start toward the authenticity with her that my fear had prevented with my dad. With gratefulness and a good bit of trepidation, I said yes.

The following week, Linda and I made our way to her house, gripping each other's hands in the car as we rode. "What do you think she will say?" Linda asked.

"No idea. She'll probably make you promise to let me go if I fall in love with a man."

We both laughed and then drove the rest of the way in silence.

My mother met us at the door and invited us to sit with her at the kitchen table. She put on water for tea and then sat down, her hands playing with the edges of the placemat in front of her. She was warm toward Linda but reserved. I felt like I had been called to the principal's office for some infraction and Linda had been an accomplice. I remember her starting with something like, "This is a bit of a surprise."

After that, I don't remember her words as much as her energy. As a child, when I did something she didn't like, she would talk more softly rather than yell. I could see she wanted to understand this, and even our presence seated together across from her seemed to help her realize that we were no different than the last time she had seen us seated next to each other— only now she knew more about just how special Linda was in my circle of friends.

Linda's straightforwardness appealed to my mother, as did her gentle way of explaining her relationship with her husband and how our connection had unfolded. She talked about meeting Joe in high school and always knowing he would be a great father—something that was important to her in a man. Joe's sister was married to her best male friend, and they spent time together as a foursome. They were intellectually matched, and he was open to her being an academic, while he was destined to become a surgeon. Everything on paper appeared to describe a dream life, but it was far more difficult living out the template than designing it in her mind.

She went on to explain that while they had wanted to be together, they were both interested in exploring other sexual experiences, and that open marriage appeared to be a viable solution—making it sound almost normal. She described how both she and Joe had had other relationships outside their marriage before this one, always with the consent of the other. My mother looked on, occasionally revealing her shock with raised eyebrows, as Linda described a marital union that was beyond her ability to fathom.

Because Linda had done everything expected of a young woman in our generation—graduate from college, get married to a doctor, and have two children—there was nothing my mother could say in objection to the life plan she had followed to date. In fact, it was the one she would have chosen for me. Yet it was flawed. Because Linda didn't suffer from any religious programming that would have made it impossible to engage in the level of freedom she had acquired, she spoke about it as a rational evolution. After the description of her open marriage, the subject of being gay seemed anticlimactic. She was sure she and Joe would part amiably with a concerted commitment to make things work for their children.

Linda spoke with the enthusiasm and conviction of an evangelist asserting the importance of family and her hopes that my mother would be a part of our new union. True to form, my mother did ask her what she would do if I fell in love with a man. Fortunately, Linda didn't let it throw her. She laughed, confident that would never happen.

We stayed for over an hour, and I could see my mother felt slightly more comfortable by the time we left. While challenges for total acceptance loomed ahead in our relationship, my mother and I had found a way to talk openly about a subject I feared might end all conversations with her. There were no more secrets between us, and I slept that night with an ease in my heart I hadn't known for decades.

belong-
ing

n January 1978, driven by a longing to find home in the big
sense—a place of belonging that I returned to every day,
where people loved and counted on me, a place signifying
permanence—I bought a house with Linda and moved in with
her and her two children.

Coming out was one thing, but coming out like this was far
beyond my knowledge and experience level. I had barely claimed
my identity as a gay woman, and now I was about to become a
gay parent. The term "blended family" had been coined just a
few years earlier, but in 1978, it didn't mean *this* blended. The
powers that be would consider this more of a scrambled family,
and not in a good way.

Custody cases favored the father if the mother was known
to be in a relationship with a woman. Anita Bryant was still on
a soapbox declaring that gays and lesbians were threatening to
our children. She clearly hadn't thought about the fact that most
gay people were the products of heterosexual coupling and had
grown up in heterosexual households. In vitro fertilization was
only in its experimental phase. Perhaps she should have worried

more about straight people. Masters and Johnson were in support of "conversion therapy" for homosexuals, asserting that they could all be "fixed." It was not a comforting environment in which to announce your bonding preference for women, let alone that you were in a *super*-blended family.

Soon I would learn that being a parent was harder than being gay. Having never babysat or changed a diaper or listened to a child scream for three hours at a time, I was completely outside my comfort zone—piloting a space shuttle to Venus would have been less daunting—and if the children hadn't been in equal portions as charming as they were exasperating, I wouldn't have made it past the first month.

As it turned out, they became two of my most important teachers about what it means to be family and for people to count on you. This was first poignantly illustrated in a series of conversations with Sara over several weeks, during drives in the car. By now, Molly was two and Sara was four. I often picked the kids up from preschool, and, long before the day of car seats, Sara would stand up in the back as I drove, usually to reprimand me for going twenty-seven miles per hour in a twenty-five miles-per-hour zone. But today she had something else on her mind. Standing up, she leaned over the front seat and, seemingly unprovoked by anything other than her own thoughts, addressed me in an authoritative voice:

"You know, Carol. You're not a part of our family."

Thanks for sharing, I thought. Since it was far from easy to take up family life as a lesbian, it was good to be put in my place by a four-year-old who made it quite clear I didn't belong there. We got home, and she asked me to cut her some salami for a snack, oblivious to my hurt feelings.

Time went on, and a week later, as I was again driving the kids home from school, and Sara, taking her usual place standing in the back seat, leaned over and said, in a more invitational tone, "Well, Carol, since you live with us, why don't you be a part of our family?" She shrugged her shoulders as though saying without words, Doesn't this seem like a reasonable thing to do?

"Sara, I would love to be a part of your family; thank you for that lovely offer." We got home, and she skipped off to play with some friends—nothing more was said about it. I sat down on the couch bemused by her comment and curious about how her thinking process had unfolded.

A few days after that, Sara and I were again driving in the car when, from her usual place, she leaned into the front seat and, in an excited voice that revealed pride in her ability to reason, said enthusiastically, "Since you live with us and are a part of our family, we should change our names to the Anderwetts!" My last name being Anderson and theirs being Hewett, she had figured out a way to merge the two and make up a new name that would formally show that we belonged together.

"That's a fabulous idea, honey," I said. "We will have to discuss it with your mom at dinner."

About a week later, when Linda and I had driven separately to visit my mother for dinner in Plymouth, Sara said she wanted to ride home with me and suggested that Molly go with her mother. We got in the car, and Sara, now buckled in the passenger's side, said eagerly, "C'mon, Carol. Let's race them home."

"That's a great idea," I said. "And I know a shortcut." I stepped on the gas, and off we went. I cut down a side street and flew as fast as the speed limit would allow. "Hang on; we're going to make a sharp turn." Sara squealed with glee, looking over her shoulder to make sure we had lost them.

"Faster, Carol, faster!" The pitch of her voice rose at every turn as she cheered me on for thirty minutes all the way home. Both of us overjoyed as we screeched into the driveway ahead of her mother and Molly, Sara blurted out, "You're the best, Carol! Why don't you and mom get married?" It was 1978, and even the shadow of such a possibility was so remote from our consciousness that no one could imagine that option in our lifetime. Yet a four-year-old had somehow, in the course of several weeks, processed the idea of home and connection and family and marriage as a totally natural conclusion for any group of people who lived together and who loved each other.

Watching Sara draw her conclusion to make me a part of her family based on love caused me to think about the arbitrary barriers adults had constructed over centuries, anchored in belief systems that overrode our basic instincts to love without judgment or conditions. I thought about the thousands of parents who lost connection with their children, of brothers and sisters who lost the companionship of their siblings, and other important family members with each other, because someone was gay. Those with the greatest privilege and power in the larger society defined the acceptable beliefs for the rest of its members, and out of those beliefs determined the norms that should be followed. Rather than listening to the voice within, people courted the voices outside of themselves, and in doing so lost touch with what most families claimed to be the most important thing: a sense of love and belonging.

I also began reframing how I identified myself. Rather than talking about my sexual orientation, I began to see my draw to women as my "love orientation." It was in relationship to women that I felt most seen, valued, and respected for the whole of me, and with that kind of love, I could most fully be myself. Sexual connection was a natural extension of intimacy, not its primary focus.

Because of the social attitudes about gays and the Christian dogma that led me to fear my own family's rejection, I never had the joy of telling my father the truth about me. The damnation from the outer world terrorized me into believing the opinion of outsiders was more powerful than my father's love and his capacity to reach beyond all of that and embrace me anyway.

Coming out to my mother showed me I had been wrong, and while it was a disappointment to her that I would never marry a man, it was one from which we both could recover. What was not possible to reclaim were the four thousand days of close connection I lost with my father in the twelve years I kept that secret from him.

chapter 17

the
struggle

Once we settled into our new family system, Linda and I set goals for ourselves. I continued my full-time job as a school psychologist and started a doctoral program in educational psychology at the University of Michigan. Linda enrolled in a PhD program in nursing and taught part-time. We were like many young families—juggling work and school and children—and we shared joint custody with Joe. We found other lesbian couples with children and built a community of support around us. We formed a group of women homeowners and taught each other how to install garbage disposals, caulk windows, and strip and refinish solid oak doors. It was empowering to be competent in the physical world and have the knowledge needed to be able to do things for ourselves instead of calling a handyman.

The first couple of years, I immersed myself in family life. To entertain the kids, I brought home a rabbit puppet that was so lifelike that people in the store came up to pet it as I nestled his nose into the crook of my arm and made him peek out at customers as I wandered through the store.

During dinner that night, I brought her to life with a shrill whiney voice as she declared, "My name is Samantha. I am here to give fines at dinner time."

"What for?" Molly asked, looking worried but intrigued.

Samantha whipped out a list of infractions that included talking with your mouth full, eating with your fingers, and not finishing your supper. And she started by penalizing Linda.

"Ohhhhhh—I saw that! I saw that!" Samantha wailed as she pointed at Linda eating a potato chip with her fingers. "Ten cents," she screamed with elation. Linda objected, "But we all eat chips with our fingers."

Samantha broke in, "Talking with your mouth full. Twenty-five cents." The kids screeched with laughter. Sam's presence at dinner kept things lively, and we posted a chart of all the fines on the refrigerator—recording penalties at each evening meal. I enjoyed making them laugh and finding my own way of relating to them that was different than the other adults who cared for them.

These moments of victory were contrasted with their random refusals to eat breakfast or lunch if their mother didn't make it, or rejections of me when I tried to read a bedtime story. Years later I discovered that those things happen with all parents and had little to do with me personally.

The second year into my PhD program, I added a master's program in film and video to my educational load, envisioning my future role as an organizational consultant making my own visual media. At the same time, my advisor introduced me to Roger Stanley, an internal consultant at Ford Motor Company, who was looking for an assistant. I won a merit scholarship and took a leave of absence from my job to attend school full-time and to work with Roger in a consulting role at Ford.

We took family vacations in Northern Michigan in the

summers, so Linda could supervise nurse practitioners in rural communities while the kids and I worked on crafts, played miniature golf, and went to the beach. On the outside, we looked like we could have been featured as a happy, successful family in *Lesbian Homes and Gardens,* had there been such a magazine.

There was a more complex, invisible story going on internally, however. While my mother and both of Linda's parents had been marginally accepting of our union, none of them were genuinely happy that their daughters were living in a gay relationship. The normal stresses of recovering from divorce and living with two children under the age of four, with both partners pursuing PhDs, were magnified by our inability to be fully "out" in every aspect of our lives or even wholly embraced by our relatives.

Tolerance is a poor substitute for acceptance, and it creates a felt need to protect yourself while working overtime to prove your worth. Had my colleagues known that Linda and I were lovers, my job as a school psychologist in a conservative community where I spent time alone in a room with children while conducting numerous psychological tests would have been in jeopardy. This very real danger eliminated the potential for support that others, freer to disclose more of their personal lives, often received from colleagues.

Most of our gay friends had one foot in the closet and one foot out, able to be open only with other gay couples or family members. We never felt entirely safe in the world, not knowing who was trustworthy in the public sphere and who was a threat. While I had grown far more comfortable with my self-acceptance, there were real risks of sharing this personal information with a broader audience. While the fact that Linda had children made everyone assume she was straight, having them in partnership with me also meant that she could be challenged in court regarding her fitness as a parent, were someone to bring such an attack. As parents we strived to support Sara's and Molly's social lives, and sometimes this meant making moral compromises that betrayed ourselves and added stress to our relationship.

One of the most telling situations arose when the parents of Molly's best friend, Jessica, offered Linda a dinner invitation. She shared the news with me during "coffee time"—the sacred hour we established without the children after dinner.

"I saw Barbara Hooper at school today when I picked Molly up, and she and Tom invited me over for dinner." The key word there was *me*, not *us*. I felt a tightness begin to form in my solar plexus. "I thought it would be good to go since Molly and Jess are such good friends."

"Are you going to tell her that you have a partner, or are you just going to go by yourself?"

"I don't think it's the right time yet—maybe after we get to know each other better."

I stared into my coffee as I spoke. "She knows you live with someone. Who does she think I am?"

"Well, the kids call you our housemate, so I'm not sure what she thinks."

Here I was again in another family, keeping a secret—hiding in plain sight. I felt my body temperature drop as more of me shrunk to fit into whatever form was necessary to garner the acceptance of others. I wasn't sure if I wanted her to tell them or not—but I was sure that I wanted her to realize the cost to us if she didn't.

Rather than turn them down or tell them the truth, Linda accepted the invitation and went solo, leaving me once again in the position of feeling invisible. Not only had they invited her for dinner, but they had asked a male friend to come, too—a man they assumed might be a good match for her to date. I

stayed home with the kids that night, sick with that old familiar feeling, like bad food decaying in my stomach. Hurt and
angry, there was no place to go with my feelings, and the ease
with which Linda seemed to accept this arrangement pained me
further. I had spent a huge part of my life concealing a defining
part of myself from others, and I didn't want to spend my future
that way, even though I rationalized the reasons for doing it.

To say my romanticized vision of becoming a super-blended
family was naive would be like saying I underestimated the size
of the ocean when I had a fantasy to swim across it. I knew nothing—about children, about transition after divorce—nothing
about parenting, and nothing about how to find my relational
place where there was already a mother and a father and where
the specter of a "real" stepmother one day joining the clan,
sanctioned as a legitimate parent through her marriage to Joe,
loomed large. Most of all, I didn't know my own personal limits
and had no grasp of the magnitude of what I was taking on,
no idea that every psychological wound of my own childhood
was a potential land mine waiting to be triggered. Nor did I
understand how the cultural context out of which I'd grown had
impacted my sense of belonging—not only to this family, but to
the wider world, as well.

Having never been in a long-term committed relationship,
I had nothing to compare this with and had no idea if it was
supposed to be this hard. The "do me, fix me, want me, take
me" life with children was exhausting. With both Linda and
me working and going to school simultaneously, there was little time to nurture our relationship, and what hours were left
in a day were taken up by the understandable neediness of a
two- and four-year-old. As is the case in most relationships, we
couldn't have known how our different families of origin had
also left unattended wounds that eventually caused ruptures in

our relationship. It was equally true that aside from her greater experience in parenting, Linda didn't know much about these things either.

To add to the already stressful dynamics alive and well in the third year of our relationship, my mother engaged me in a conversation over lunch one afternoon about Christmas. It began with her usual question.

"What are your plans for the holiday? I've been thinking of going to Florida to spend time with Jerry." Her sister had moved there several years earlier, and my mother, wanting to create some new traditions since my father's death, had started to spend holidays away from home.

"I'm sure we will spend some time up north with Linda's folks and then some time with you, if you're around."

My mother sat in the booth across from me, her sandwich held in both hands as she leaned forward to take a bite. Staring at the food instead of me, she off-handedly said, "Well, I wanted to let you know that I'm not buying presents this year for anyone who isn't a part of our family." I could feel my face scrunch up as I looked at her, trying to figure out what she was telling me. "I don't have as much money this year, so I won't be buying Linda a present, but I will get the kids something."

I cocked my head to one side and listened especially hard. Was my mother really declaring to me that she didn't consider Linda a part of our family? And was she asking me to believe that this somehow made sense? That it was reasonable and rational—not something to which I would take offense when she had gotten her presents in the past? To understand the full weight of this message, one would have to know that my mother loved buying Christmas presents, that it wouldn't be unusual for her to purchase a gift for the bagger at Kroger's supermarket, if the spirit moved her, or for the mailman, or the pharmacist at

Woods Drugs. She was consistently the most generous person I knew. And, of course, she would get my brother's wife, Laurie, something because she *was* a part of our family.

My ears burned with rage at this announcement, my hands knotted in fists beneath the table as if to keep the steam from rising through my body and out of my ears. But beneath that roiling fire was hurt and sadness. I sat quietly for a minute or so, trying to quell the beast inside that wanted to lacerate her with words, to scream, to swear, to condemn the un-Christian nature of her statement. Instead, I swallowed hard and said, "Well, Laurie is no more a part of our family than Linda is. It is the law that makes her so—not her DNA." Then I stood up to leave and said, as I walked away, "If you're that hard up for money, don't buy me a present either." I got in my car and felt my whole body constrict. If what she said was true, I had no family—not the one I was born into and not the one Linda and I were trying to shape.

A few days later, my mother called as though nothing had happened, but I wasn't about to let this go. "You know, Mom, you really hurt my feelings when you said you weren't going to buy a present for Linda. She is my family, and we want you to be a part of it, but it's not all right to treat her that way."

"Oh, honey, you know I would never do that."

"Well, if you would never do that, then don't ever say you would."

Even without seeing her in person, I could tell she felt sheepish about what she had done and that she wanted to take it back. Hard as I tried to let it go completely, it was like being stung by a bee—even after the bee flies away, the stinger is left behind in your body along with the venom it carried. In the end, she bought Linda a beautiful gift, but my joy in that had been muted long before that moment.

⁘

Halfway through my master's program in film and video, I won a national competition for an internship in Hollywood offered by the Academy of Television Arts and Sciences. I would live there for six weeks in the summer, work with a video tape editor, and share in group activities with the fifteen other interns from around the country who had been selected for other production specialties like sound recording or film making. Worried that the kids would be affected by such a long absence, I wrote them daily letters, plastering images and stickers all over them in place of words—mini-collages they could look forward to in the mail. I also sent them small gifts over the six weeks to let them know I was thinking about them. It was 1982, and we didn't have cell phones, Skype, FaceTime, or any technology of convenience that made it easier to stay in touch. I also called every day to talk, though their interest in those connections was fleeting, and they frequently dashed off after a few words of greeting.

Even though I missed the routine of home, I loved being alone again—on my own and not responsible for anyone but me. That feeling of freedom was a relief from the unending stress of responsibility I felt. Yet I couldn't imagine ever leaving them, bound by love and loyalty to two children who hadn't asked for me to be a part of their lives and who would surely suffer again if Linda and I were to split up. I didn't really know how they were processing my temporary absence, but I wanted to make sure they knew I was with them even though we were apart.

Linda joined me for the last two weeks of my trip. The joy we once found in the ease of long evenings together by the fire in my apartment was more frequently replaced with short tempers and conflicting needs. My desire to have a few days alone to focus on each other conflicted with her need to be in more continuous connection with the kids. There was no time even when we were away to completely refresh the passionate feelings that initially drew us together. We quarreled much of the time we were in California, and each of us was happy to come home. After a month and a half of absence, I was eager to see the kids again and imagined them running to the door to greet me especially upon our return. Instead, Sara gave a quick embrace as she brushed by me to greet her mother and then went outside to play with a friend. Molly sat at the top of the stairs and refused to come down. In fact, she ignored me for more than a week as I endeavored to re-establish my relationship with her. Over time, while I remained bewildered, we returned to our daily routine, and things came round to normal.

Two months later, on my birthday in November, Molly presented me with a hand-made card. On the front, my name was spelled in large print. Beneath that was a full-frontal picture of an elephant with a balloon above his head that said "Hi."

On the inside in her best printing were scrawled the words:

I will be your pall [sic] but you have to like me. I hope you never leave again. I know everybody loves you. But I love you better. From Molly.

I sat in the rocker in the living room absorbing the unexpected power of her words. Her seven-year-old brain registered in black-and-white conclusions about my absence and her importance in my life in a way that gripped me. It was a great lesson that one never really knows what goes on in the mind and heart of someone else—especially a child.

Eventually Linda and I enlisted the support of a therapist. Neither of us had a full understanding of our issues and we had even less ability to effectively address them. On our first evening, we faced a slightly overweight, stern-looking colleague of Linda's who had a degree in clinical psychology. She sat across from us, arms folded, and opened the session with, "What can I do for you?"

My instinctive response was, "You could start by smiling." While I wanted the help, we both were too vulnerable to open up to our deepest feelings, so that foray into enlightenment was brief and not very beneficial. Shortly after that, we found another therapist and worked away at the surface issues—children, money, freedom, jealousy, time—but we never got to the understanding we needed about how our original family dynamics played out in our relationship and the responsibility each of us had to comprehend and change those. Instead, we organized our weekly arguments to show the therapist why the other person was totally at fault.

After five years, the strain was too great. Linda became attracted to someone else, just as she graduated with her doctorate, and was eager to move on. By then, I had finished all of my course work for my PhD and taken my prelims. I was also graduating with my master's in film and video. It was disheartening that all of our hopefulness had come to this, and I wondered how any couple, whether straight or gay, managed to navigate the seemingly overwhelming challenges of a primary relationship. As much as I wanted a home and a family, I had a lot to learn about how to bring this desire to fruition.

The hardest part was leaving the kids, not only from my concern about the impact of this second loss on them, but also because I had grown to love them as my own. Sara was nine and Molly was seven the night I drove up to the house to tell them, with Linda, that we were splitting up. Walking into the dining room, I felt a swirl of emotions—sadness, anger, despair, resignation. We all sat in the dining room while Linda explained that we were not going to be together anymore. The words dropped into the hollow place inside of me that had been carved out after years of misunderstanding between us. As I watched them watch her, my hand tightened around the yellow paper from the legal pad upon which I had carefully printed them a goodbye letter. They were so small and vulnerable—standing in their rumpled play clothes. The confusion on their faces was evident—unable to take in the meaning of it all until the tears appeared at the corners of their eyes and they glanced at me, looking for confirmation or hope for some sign that there might be a mistake.

When Linda finished, Sara and Molly came over to where I sat on the small fold-out couch; each grabbed me around my neck as my arms encircled their tiny frames, my eyes staring out the window across the dining room table, focused on the swing set we had assembled the first year we moved in. We all cried, smooshed up together in a big ball, holding on tightly. It was impossible to know how they were processing this. When the sniffling stopped, I got up from the couch and asked them to sit down. I kneeled in front of them and slowly read my letter, explaining in simple language that their mother and I still loved each other, but our differences were too great to work things out. I promised to love them forever and told them they would always be my children in a special way—that our parting had nothing to do with them.

Then I reached into a bag where I had kept Samantha and pulled her out.

"I want you to have her because you are the ones who brought her to life." Molly reached out her hands and grabbed Sam by the neck and clutched her to her chest. She had always been especially fond of this magical rabbit—so much so that I had gotten her a smaller version of Sam for her birthday, which she named Cherries. Now the mother and daughter bunnies would be together forever.

They got off the couch, and we hugged once more, as tightly as the moment before. Letting go of them was the hardest task in my life so far, feeling the weight of chosen responsibility to never leave them emotionally, even though we would never live together again. The only thing that would make them believe my words would be to prove it with my actions—a promise I knew I would keep.

We said goodbye at the door, and I moved slowly down the steps, got in my car, and drove around the streets of Ann Arbor for an hour, sobbing, until I made my way back to a friend's house where I was staying until I could find an apartment.

While I was out to many in our community, I was not out to everyone at school or at work. Once again, my grief took place alone—out of my fear people would see our breakup either as a positive thing, because they were against gays, or as inevitable for people living a lifestyle not accepted as the norm. People would expect us to fail. My feelings were too raw to risk reaching out for any potential comfort I might gain by sharing the sadness of our breakup, for fear there would be even greater negative consequences for revealing that we were domestic partners. Not knowing who would be sympathetic, I suffered by myself, out of view from anyone who might not understand. I think my mother was secretly hopeful this failure would turn me around and invite me to reconsider being with men. She never said that, and she did her best to offer support, but mostly I felt alone. My work was taking more of my time, and Linda "got" the softball team in our split, leaving me more socially isolated.

Linda's and my relationship had been the first real one I'd had as an adult in which I was not second-guessing whether I should be with a man or wondering what people would think about my being with a woman. I learned things I should have been able to explore in my twenties, but because of my anguished ambivalence about whom I could love, I had never focused on how to love another person as a life partner. While a relationship with a woman did not ensure success, I had no question that being with a woman was right for me.

chapter 18

alone and free

Both Linda and I graduated with honors in April 1982. I had completed my prelims for my PhD in educational psychology and had attained my master's in film and video. Linda had finished her doctorate in nursing. In spite of the great success we had achieved in meeting our educational goals, we had failed in our ability to sustain and grow our relationship.

Seated in the audience on graduation day, we were separated not only by the geography of our assigned classes, but also by the emotional gulf that had widened over the five years it took to achieve our respective accomplishments. As my eyes gazed across the crowd of thirteen thousand graduates and guests, I wondered about the lives of all the others parading across the stage to get their long-sought-after diplomas. What had been lost to them in pursuit of this dream? While school was not the primary reason for our breakup, it certainly added additional stress. I imagined we weren't alone in that. Were all the others in the audience as happy as they looked, or were they suffering in some way beneath their nicely pressed black gowns, faces arranged in permanent smiles?

On a day we had planned and struggled to claim together with joy, raising our glasses of champagne, she was embarking on a new life with someone else, while I was starting out again on my own. Most of all, the years together had taught me that before I entered into any relationship with someone new, I needed to know myself far better than I did right now, and that became my primary focus going forward.

Just prior to graduation, I had moved out of the house into a small apartment a mile away. Linda's new love moved into the house we owned together and paid me rent for the half that was mine. Some friends came and helped me transfer my belongings along with a few pieces of furniture to my new living space. I got the dog, Casey, in the dissolution of our partnership, and she, of course, got the children.

My one new acquisition for my apartment was a waterbed that I had been coveting for some time, and, in an effort to console myself, I made the purchase. In spite of my exhaustion on moving day, I pressed forward, filled up the mattress with water, and made the bed before putting a few more things away. An hour later, as I readied myself to sleep, I pulled back the covers and noticed they felt damp around the edges. As I slid my fingers down the inside of the liner, I felt a faint touch of moisture. It was not a lot—just enough to let me know there was a leak somewhere. What were the odds that the full 158 gallons would gush out before morning, I wondered.

By now, it was midnight, and I was completely out of steam, out of patience, out of luck. My brain furiously scanned for possible options. I registered that there were two: either get out the hose and drain the mattress right now, or turn out the light, pray for mercy, and sleep on the couch. I chose the latter, grabbed my pillow, and traipsed back out to the living room, where I lay down on the black vinyl sofa. Casey followed my lead and jumped up beside me, and we both slept until morning. Fortunately the leak was small and I was able to find and fix it before any serious damage was done. I only hoped this was not an omen for life on my own.

While I had no formal rights regarding time with the children, both Linda and Joe knew we had a special bond and they were both supportive of my spending time with them. On their first visitation, they wanted to make chocolate chip cookies. I had no baking supplies or pans in the house as all of that had been left for Linda, so I rose early and went to the store. By the time I was finished I had spent twenty-five dollars on all the paraphernalia needed for this special engagement.

Linda dropped them off later that morning, and they ran to the door, greeting me with hugs that lingered for minutes. My arms surrounded them both as we dragged each other from the doorway into the kitchen. On the table, neatly arranged, were the chocolate chips, the unsalted butter, the dark brown sugar, eggs, vanilla extract, flour, and baking soda. Molly eyed the chips and ripped them open to make sure they were edible.

For an hour I watched them measure and pour the ingredients into the new sparkling bowls and use all their strength to mush everything together, fighting over whose turn it was to put in the next ingredient. My heart ached with the knowledge that they would grow up without me in their daily lives, and while living with them had been the most challenging thing I had ever done, leaving them was even more difficult.

They stayed the whole day, devouring multiple samples of their product until their dad came to pick them up. After he had settled them in the car and as I cleaned up the mess left behind, I heard a knock at the door. Joe had returned, and I motioned him to come in.

"I want you to know how much it means to me that you are

staying connected to the kids," he said. "They think the world of you, and I know they miss you." He leaned forward and gave me a hug, then turned around and left. My heart was heavy and light. Their absence left an unfillable void, but his words lifted me with hope, and his generosity in sharing them carried me forward with the faith we would stay in touch far into the future.

The same month I finished school, my mentor, Roger, invited me to work on another project, this one outside of Ford at a paper mill in South Carolina. My one-year leave of absence as a school psychologist was up, and I needed to decide if I was going to return or not. If I accepted Roger's offer, I would have to quit my job permanently, yet he could promise me no more than forty days of work. It was a choice between security and my dream of being a consultant. The timing was awful, given my new living situation and the uncertainty of any future financial opportunities, yet this project was completely enticing. It was focused on the design and implementation of an employee-involvement program for all the hourly workers in the plant. The approach was based on a newly embraced and effective concept in organizational development, in which a group of employees met regularly to identify, analyze, and solve work-related problems. The goals were improving performance and motivating employees through meaningful involvement with the things that affected them.

As I weighed the pros and cons, I remembered that the risk I had taken in leaving my job as a teacher to go back to school had proven to be among the best of my life. It had not only opened me up to new work, but also put me on the path toward owning my sexuality and finding peace within. There had not really been a downside, in spite of my initial worries. The hardest part, as always, would be telling my mother.

I got through the conversation with Mom, reminding her of her oft-repeated phrase to me when she once left employment—"I was looking for a job when I found this one." In fact, it was her boldness in the face of challenge that had been an inspiration throughout my life, and she had faced difficulties far greater than mine. It was curious to me that she didn't grasp the contradiction between the way she lived her life and the advice she often gave me.

Before accepting his offer and quitting my job, I knew I had to tell Roger that I was gay. I was through hiding, and though I didn't find it necessary to tell everyone, I wasn't going to keep it a secret from people with whom I was close—especially not a colleague who was offering me a coveted opportunity to partner with him on a new project. In spite of my resolve, I was quite nervous about the pending conversation. Roger was a former Catholic priest who left the order because he wanted to marry. While this suggested he had made some hard choices in his own life, I had no idea what his views were on homosexuality and how they might affect his desire to work with me. What if he thought it was an unforgivable sin? What if he wouldn't want to be associated with me? I would lose out on an extraordinary chance to learn the consulting business while working with someone I respected. What if he decided to tell others at Ford and I lost some of those clients as well? All the old fears came rolling back the closer I came to having the talk. But now there was no alternative in my life but for me to tell the truth.

We sat across the white pressboard tables at Afternoon Delight after placing our order for salads. This was the meeting where he would fill me in on the details of the project and the schedule for our workshops and set meeting times for us to develop the design together. Roger was his usual upbeat self, dressed in his khaki pants and button-down blue oxford shirt. His short gray hair was perfectly combed as he peered at me through his oversize wire-rimmed glasses—his smile revealing the gap between his two front teeth.

"I'm delighted you are going to work on this project with me," he said as he looked around for the silverware that was back at the salad bar. "I think you're ready to do something more substantial." He got up and retrieved his utensils and then returned.

I thought I'd better dive right in before I lost my nerve. "I'm honored that you asked me, and I'm very eager to take on greater responsibility." I pierced one of the tomatoes with my fork and went on. "Before we talk further about the details of the engagement, I want to tell you something about myself so you aren't ever blindsided by it." He looked up, put his silverware down, and gave me his full attention. "I want you to know that I'm gay, and I know from experience that that can be a concern for some people, and I just want to make sure it is not a concern for you." Short and simple, I had said it. Now I held my breath, awaiting his response.

"That doesn't bother me," he said without a moment's contemplation. "Is that Ranch dressing on your salad? Where'd you get that?" I pointed to the side table next to salad bar, and he went off to find some. When he returned, he thanked me for telling him, and we moved on to the agenda for the meeting.

His response was a reassuring surprise. I don't know what I had expected. I only knew telling him was the right thing to do. It made me curious how many others might have been as nonchalant and accepting about my revelation as he was. How many meaningful relationships had I passed over or denied out of my fear to share this information with them? What losses, besides my father, had I suffered? Even if the steps were small at first, they would be in the direction of truth and authenticity. I felt proud of myself for telling him.

I loved the work at the paper mill in Charleston, and because Roger was still employed at Ford, he often sent me alone to work with the client when he couldn't get off. My early success at Ford with union members was a great education in understanding the politics of large organizations and in winning the trust and respect of people, regardless of their level in the system. I had a special fondness for hourly workers, as my dad had been one for years while employed at the Rouge Plant—a part of the Ford Motor Company complex. Sometimes I imagined him sitting in a group that I facilitated and wondered how he would have responded to the new ideas being proposed. I pondered what he would have thought of me standing at the front, recording his opinions on a flip chart, as the group worked to solve a problem.

One day, close to a year into the project, which, to my enormous relief, had grown substantially based on the success of the first forty days, Roger took me aside. "I need to tell you something that I think will really upset you. Let's go somewhere private." My gut twisted with worry as we made our way through the cacophony of paper machines that rolled on in the background, passing men in hard hats and overalls splattered with dirt from crawling on the ground under the giant rollers to do routine maintenance. Following Roger, eyes straight ahead, reminded me of the night David escorted me to his office, after canceling the class I was teaching, to relay the news that my father had died. I could almost hear the clack of my boot heels striking the tile floor as similar thoughts raced through my head. Was I in trouble? Had I said something out of line to one of the men? Was the president of the company upset with me?

We turned the corner and entered the conference room, sparsely furnished with a small Formica table and three plastic chairs. The walls were bare with the exception of a large laminated poster listing safety rules in bold black print. He pointed to a seat and then sat kitty-corner from me. I fidgeted with my pen and notebook awaiting his words. Roger looked up as though reluctant to tell me. Finally, he leaned forward and said, "Barry, the HR guy, is spreading rumors that you are gay."

Surprisingly, I sensed my body relaxing. I exhaled and felt a smile come across my face. "Wow, what a relief. I thought you were going to tell me that people were unhappy with my work." My reaction was a shock even to me. I had spent so much of my life in fear, especially careful to create the false impression that I was straight, that I was "normal," that I belonged—in the stilted way one never can, when they are pretending. I had felt on many occasions that my life would be over if people knew the truth, that I would be shunned, damned, flung out of the kingdom, forever banished. The terror was so real it had made me guarded in all aspects of my life. I was careful in the words I chose, the activities I shared, the way I arranged my house, the people I invited over. It was a tidy external construction, yet I had created a prison with invisible bars that had constricted my interactions with others for decades.

At last, my *genuine* reaction was to be more concerned about what people thought of my work than their assumptions about my lifestyle. While revealing myself to Roger had been an enormous step, this was the ultimate reward. It was true I was gay and that I had no control over what people thought about that. I only had control over how I showed up in the world as a person and whether or not people could experience the value I brought to any situation. My response was a blinding revelation to me of how far I had come. I was giddy. The thing that had once scared me the most was no longer a threat to my existence.

I knew I had gained the respect of the men and women with whom I was working and felt confident this would not jeopardize my relationships. I was especially glad now that I had told Roger in advance. He had chosen me based on my ability to do the job he needed, and that was all that mattered to him. The rumor faded from circulation as quickly as it had flashed into the open; the mutual respect between these employees and myself was the abiding antidote to that poison.

The work with Roger expanded significantly. Within a couple of years he left his job at Ford while I retained a few clients in different departments there. Soon I had my own thriving business as an organizational consultant, strengthened by other clients outside of Ford that I had earned through word-of-mouth successes and new contracts with Roger.

Most importantly, I took a nine-year hiatus from a long-term commitment with anyone. This time was spent getting to know myself, what I wanted and needed in a relationship, what I was willing and able to give. The gift of all these years of struggle through relationships with both genders was to become a woman who loved herself as she was. I reclaimed the pride my father always had in me, and I knew he would be cheering me on, gratified by my courage to finally stand up for what I believed in, to become the adult he had always seen in the child he nurtured with his unceasing faith and love. I still had a long way to go to heal the scars inflicted by a fundamentalist paradigm and to feel safe in the world to which

I was born. But I could go forward with greater peace in my heart and a compassionate understanding of the forces that had shaped my past, certain I had become the artist who would craft her own future.

you can't buy love like that

My mother and I were in the fourteenth year of our monthly ritual of meeting for breakfast at the Big Boy restaurant. While she would still ask periodically if I was interested in meeting some guy at her church, she had generally accepted the fact that her hopes for a son-in-law would never come to fruition, and a greater tranquility had settled between us. Most importantly, there were no longer secrets that kept us apart.

She shared her diagnosis of cancer in November of 1992. It wasn't life-threatening, the doctor said, because it was caught so early. She'd undergo a small operation to remove a few inches of her colon, and she would be as good as new. At eighty-four, it didn't turn out that way. In his single-minded focus on the cancer, the doctor overlooked the deeper cause of her difficulties: scleroderma, an autoimmune rheumatic disease. She continued to decline after the operation, making multiple trips to the emergency room through the winter, often because of congestive heart failure.

On February 28, 1993, I made my usual trip to St. Joseph Mercy Hospital to visit her, a fistful of roses in my hand to brighten her room. When I arrived, one of the many specialists was finishing his exam, but he let me stay. Standing at a distance, I watched her lying under crisp white sheets staring past the thirty-year-old boy-man playing doctor. He sat upright on her bed, all starched and stiff with shiny oxfords and a pale pink shirt, writing with a black Pilot Razor pen. "Mrs. Anderson," he shouted, as though my mother were deaf and not dying of cancer. "Do you know what day it is?"

She squinted to see the calendar that hung beyond his left shoulder, rolled her eyes as though reflecting, and said, "Either the twenty-seventh or twenty-eighth of February." It was the weekend, and the days were split in half on the yellow paper across the room. He nodded, acknowledging her answer, and then he went on to reframe the question.

"What day of the week is it?"

She squinted again and said, "Saturday or Sunday."

In that moment I felt such love for her, all frayed around the edges of wrinkled skin that no longer fit like a tight wet suit. I watched her eyes—they shut, lashes curled down, as the man rose from the bed and left the room. When she heard the door close behind him, she opened one eye and glanced in my direction, and we joined each other in a giggle.

I sat on her bed and held her hand. Somewhere between thinking she would live forever and realizing that forever was here, I was hit with a wave of grief. Even after months of hospital treatments, late-night visits to the ER, and midday calls to her in-home nurse, my denial had been intact. But today was different. I could see that it took effort for her to lift her hand to rest it in mine and noticed her eyelids closed unexpectedly as she dozed off in the middle of a sentence. Her breathing was labored. Somehow I had expected more warning—that there would be an announcement the last time we were in line at Big

Boy's restaurant for cold bacon and crispy burnt toast at the all-you-can-eat buffet that it really was the last time. That after she came in September to spend the night at my house on Berkley Street, she would never come again. That eating Russian tea-cakes and drinking Constant Comment at her kitchen table was a monthly ritual never to be repeated.

Now, all of those ordinary moments took on a sacred quality.

She woke up again, and I helped her to sit up. "Hi, dear," she said in her usual strong voice. "Hand me that water, please, my mouth is so dry." She strained forward to grasp the cup in her hands and took a sip through the straw.

I had come early to the hospital so I could spend time alone with her, knowing friends from church would soon arrive after the morning service. The day before, I had pulled the doctor aside and asked the frightful question: "How long does she have?"

While I wanted to hear him say, "She is going to be fine; it's just a little hump to get over," I knew that was a fantasy. He responded instead, with the chilling words, "Probably six months."

I asked if we should make arrangements for hospice, and he agreed. Nodding his head as an indication he really needed to get someplace else, he turned and left me standing there.

I walked over to the window and looked out at the parking lot. The world appeared so orderly from the fifth floor looking down—automobiles were aligned in perfect rows, the roadways leading up to the hospital looked like veins leading to the heart, small cars motoring on them like blood pumping life into the monolithic structure in which I stood. Everything inside of me felt disorderly, like a trashcan blown over in the wind. The only positive thing was that we would have more time.

Though my mother wasn't present for that conversation, she was aware her days were numbered. More pragmatic than anyone I knew, once she had the facts of any situation, no matter how grave, she was straightforward in her acceptance, without question and without drama.

She sat up straighter in the bed and in her usual animated way said, "I've had a great life, you know, and haven't we had fun?" She grinned and shook her head, reminiscing about the time she relented and bought me a saber saw for my birthday, when she would have preferred to give me a new dress. And the time she caved, after my relentless pleading, to buy me hiking boots for Christmas instead of the faux pearl necklace she had in mind.

"What about the diet doctor?" I chimed in. "And those great corned beef sandwiches at Billie's? And remember when you hung my Raggedy Ann doll in the overhead light that burned all her hair off and you performed a skin graft operation on the kitchen table?"

"What about the time you went on a bike trip to China?" she countered, making a frightful face. "And when you quit your teaching job and went back to graduate school? You're something else," she added, with a half smile as she pointed her index finger at me and shook it as though she were scolding me. I had witnessed that gesture often, a mixture of alarm and admiration for my risk-taking nature: a final acceptance of the ways in which we were fundamentally different.

Then she stopped laughing and grew serious. "You know, when you told me you were gay, I told Dr. Barnard, the minister at my church, and he said not to tell anyone because they wouldn't accept you."

She had never mentioned this to me before, and I hadn't known that she had ever told anyone. Then she went on, eyes fixed on mine.

"I want you to know, honey, that I didn't need for you to be with a man to be a better person than you are—I needed that for me."

I stood there not knowing what to say. I had waited fifteen years to hear some version of those words—to know that in her heart my mother had always seen me for my character and was proud of me as her daughter.

"As long as you accepted me, that was all that mattered," I said quietly, returning her gaze.

"I know that now."

I walked to the side of the bed and touched her hand, then silently traced the river of veins on top as I slid my palm beneath hers. She looked at me for a moment and then closed her eyes. I closed mine, too, and felt the slight weight of her hand in mine.

The boy-doctor had said it would be six months, but it was less than a week. My mother came home from the hospital in an ambulance one day after our conversation, climbed up on the hospice bed that we'd placed in the living room of her home, and started her departure to the world beyond. It was so like her. I could almost hear her say, "My time is up. I'm leaving now."

I was settling in for a longer vigil, weeks and months to sit by her side and together remember all the special moments of the past. We would have time to drift apart slowly, and I could let go a little more each day. But it seemed like only hours before she began floating in and out of a coma, prompting me to call my brother, Jim, in Georgia. I told him the time was short and he needed to come.

I reached out to my closest friends in Seattle and California, as well as the ones nearby, and they assembled in random shifts around the clock for the next three days. I sat on the yellow-patterned sofa during breaks from the bedside and reflected on my mother's life. Flashbacks streamed before me like snapshots on a slide carousel out of control: my brother and me in the little red wagon when we were three and five; her baking, cake batter all over the counter and the smell of chocolate chip cookies beckoning me forward; her voice calling me home at night from ice-skating in the park at the end of our street; her pride in my losing forty-three pounds when I was fifteen; the look on her face when I gave her a hundred-dollar bill to pay off her charge card for Mother's Day; my sweet-sixteen party; her surprise eightieth-birthday celebration.

Waiting for death was like living in a Salvador Dali painting, each transition both expected and surprising. I watched her drift back and forth in and out of consciousness and listened for the rattle in her breathing that comes when death is imminent, leaping up from the couch each time her rhythm shifted. I was wearing the same clothes I had donned two days before, fearful she would depart if I left even for minutes to take a shower.

Late on the final day, she stirred and in a whisper said, "My feet feel like they are tied together."

I came close to her bed and touched her on the shoulder. "They aren't, Mom," I said softly, "they probably just feel that way."

It was the first time I heard a hint of fearfulness in her voice. She was the most radically stoic person I knew. In spite of all the strength she demonstrated throughout her life, it occurred to me that beneath her deep belief in God and heaven and life beyond the physical plane, there was still a vast unknown yet to be discovered, and in this moment, she might not be so sure she could trust what was next.

I climbed up on the hospice bed, lay down next to her, and stroked her forehead as I spoke. "I am going to go with you all the way to the other side, Mom."

She turned her head toward me, her eyes still closed, and whispered, "You can't buy love like that."

ACKNOWLEDGEMENTS

Writing a book is a community effort, and I couldn't have done it without the support of my family, friends, mentors, and colleagues who read early chapters, offered helpful feedback, encouraged me when I was lost, and never doubted I would finish.

Special appreciation goes to the following:

My parents, for modeling strong character and unshakable courage in everyday actions—for showing me how to do hard things with love.

Archer Christian, the love of my life, for your fierce belief in my story, your keen editing eye, and your ability to quell my fears with your unwavering belief in me.

Mauree McKaen, my lifelong friend. You told me forty years ago that I should write a book because you thought I had something to say. Thank you for holding that vision until I caught up to it.

My mentors—Jacob Levinson, Diana Hume George, Maddy Blais, and Suzannah Lassard—who called me a writer and made me believe I was one.

Kay Gould Caskey and Jim Johnston, for creating safety and offering courage for emerging writers to find their voice.

My book club pals—Jane Dutton, Laurie Lachance, Rita Benn, and Amy Saunders. You insisted we read my manuscript and wowed me with your feedback and encouragement—even before the wine.

Brooke Warner and Linda Joy Myers, for having an online course called *Kickstart Your Memoir*, which gave me the courage to start and the tools that helped me finish.

Magic and R. K. for bringing light, laughter, and beauty to each day—for showing me what it means to belong.

ABOUT THE AUTHOR

photo credit: Anne Keesor

Carol E. Anderson is a life coach and former organizational consultant. She has traveled the world extensively for work and pleasure—most recently to Kenya on a photo safari and to the Democratic Republic of the Congo on a philanthropic mission. She holds a doctorate in spiritual studies, and master's degrees in psychology, organizational development, and creative nonfiction. She is the founder of Rebellious Dreamers, an eighteen-year-strong non-profit organization that has helped women over thirty-five realize dreams they'd deferred and women of all ages come into their own. Anderson is the author of the essay "What Is it About Memoir?," published in *The Magic of Memoir*, and coauthor of "Deeper Power," published in *Enlightened Power: How Women are Transforming the Practice of Leadership*. This is her first memoir. She lives with the love of her life and their sassy pup in a nature sanctuary in Ann Arbor, MI.

SELECTED TITLES FROM SHE WRITES PRESS

She Writes Press is an independent publishing company founded to serve women writers everywhere.
Visit us at **www.shewritespress.com**.

Uncovered: How I Left Hassidic Life and Finally Came Home by Leah Lax. $16.95, 978-1-63152-995-5. Drawn in their offers of refuge from her troubled family and promises of eternal love, Leah Lax becomes a Hassidic Jew—but ultimately, as a forty-something woman, comes to reject everything she has lived for three decades in order to be who she truly is.

Blue Apple Switchback: A Memoir by Carrie Highley. $16.95, 978-1-63152-037-2. At age forty, Carrie Highley finally decided to take on the biggest switchback of her life: upon her bicycle, and with the help of her mentor's wisdom, she shed everything she was taught to believe as a young lady growing up in the South—and made a choice to be true to herself and everyone else around her.

All the Ghosts Dance Free: A Memoir by Terry Cameron Baldwin. $16.95, 978-1-63152-822-4. A poetic memoir that explores the legacy of alcoholism and teen suicide in one woman's life—and her efforts to create an authentic existence in the face of that legacy.

The S Word by Paolina Milana. $16.95, 978-1-63152-927-6. An insider's account of growing up with a schizophrenic mother, and the disastrous toll the illness—and her Sicilian Catholic family's code of secrecy—takes upon her young life.

The Space Between: A Memoir of Mother-Daughter Love at the End of Life by Virginia A. Simpson. $16.95, 978-1-63152-049-5. When a life-threatening illness makes it necessary for Virginia Simpson's mother, Ruth, to come live with her, Simpson struggles to heal their relationship before Ruth dies.

Times They Were A-Changing: Women Remember the '60s & '70s edited by Kate Farrell, Amber Lea Starfire, and Linda Joy Myers. $16.95, 978-1-938314-04-9. Forty-eight powerful stories and poems detailing the breakthrough moments experienced by women during the '60s and '70s.